Hillbilly
in the
Real Estate Jungle

Front cover design by Stephen W. White.

Hillbilly in the Real Estate Jungle

With 59 Lessons Gained by Personal Experience

Joseph C. White

Rockville, Maryland

Hillbilly in the Real Estate Jungle

Joseph C. White
9900 Silver Brook Drive
Rockville, MD 20850
http://www.josephcwhite.com

ISBN 0-9726095-0-4
Published January 2003

Published in the United States of America by:
Crossing Trails
4804 Kentwood Lane
Woodbridge, VA 22193
http://www.crossingtrails.com

This book is dedicated to my wife Linda
and all my children, who have all
helped, along with my success
in real estate, to make my senior years
some of the happiest of my life.

I also want to recognize and thank
my friends and relatives who
encouraged me to write this book.

And thanks to Harold Nesbitt, my editor
and publisher, whose expertise and
guidance made this book possible.

Joseph C. White, Realtor®, 1985

Foreword

Since this is an autobiography of a certain part of my life, I am writing in my own voice and in the first person. I may thus be accused of self aggrandizement, but all the stories are as factual as my memory can recall, and I have neither exaggerated nor embellished them.

This is neither a how-to-get-rich article on real-estate investing, nor a textbook of correct real-estate practices. And it certainly makes no claim to literary elegance. This is simply an account, in my own country words, of my experiences as a real-estate agent, as a homeowner, as a landlord, and as an investor. I ran into many difficulties they would never have told me about in school or in the instruction books.

You may be assured that things will not always go smoothly, and now and then something or somebody will cause you heartburn. If you want to know about the kind of problems you are likely to encounter and how to survive them, then read this book.

Mine is not a spectacular success story such as those of thousands who have made it big in real estate or in other fields. Neither is it a testimonial for some mail order system for getting rich quickly in real estate with no prior knowledge, no money, no credit, and with very little effort. The ads for those systems remind me of a description I once heard of a Texas longhorn: "A point here, a point there, and a lot of bull in between."

This is merely the story of the oldest son of a church-mouse-poor family of row-cropping dirt farmers in Tennessee during the great depression. Of a man who did more hard, dirty, and disagreeable work as a teenager than most men do in a lifetime.

But out of that tough country crucible came a feeling of pride and independence and a determination to succeed that paid off in later years. It helped me to muddle through and persevere to financial independence through real estate investments, learning many valuable lessons in the process.

I started this odyssey recently out of the military and fresh off the farm, selling cheap little houses for small down payments. In three or four years I progressed to selling new houses built by a construction company, but still small houses with small down payments. Then, during 21 years working for the federal government, I bought and sold several houses and four apartment buildings. After retirement, it was back to real estate, and I completed the Realtors Institute courses, passed the required five-week-long study courses for the Commercial Investment Member designation, took a course is appraising, and took a course in syndication. The story continues to my full retirement and includes estate planning for my heirs.

To summarize, I made an $800 signature loan from a credit union in 1957 for the down payment on a small brick house in Fairfax County, Virginia. Three years later, I transferred to Puerto Rico. We couldn't sell on short notice, so we rented it to cover the mortgage payments. Nine years later, in 1966, we sold and got 10 times the down payment, which we used to rehab a 12-unit apartment building in Richmond, Virginia. We had bought it with 100 percent financing by making a formal commitment to make certain improvements within 90 days. We converted it to 18 units, and eight years later, we sold that building and got a cashier's check for 10 times that down payment, or 100 times the initial investment in the little house. We used that as the down payment on a 30-unit apartment building in Florida, assuming a first mortgage and giving a second mortgage for the balance. From a divorce in 1978, I got full ownership as my part of an amicable property settlement.

In 1982 I "mortgaged out" (refinanced the second mortgage and took out more cash than the down payment had been.) I had back the initial investment in the Richmond building plus all the profit from the sale. The equity in the 30 units was mine for free.

I kept adjusting rents to keep up with the market and, as a result, sold the property in 1983 for a million dollars, more than twice what I had paid for it. Pursuant to our contract, the buyer paid off the second mortgage, and I took back a purchase-money second mortgage for more than the total price I paid for the building in the first place. The profits and income from that building and from the mortgage will pay more than both my wife and I have earned in our lifetimes from all the jobs we ever had.

"If you are lucky enough," my father used to say, "sawdust will do for brains." I never claimed to be really smart, so I guess *sawdust worked for me.*

Along the way, I had a running battle with IRS over a $900 assessment for additional taxes, and eventually won it without the help of a lawyer. Later, I was faced with the probability of taking back a property I had sold, and had to spend several hundred dollars with four different lawyers before I could find out for sure what the total tax consequences of foreclosing would be.

Still later, I was involved in a three-hour arbitration session concerning a foreclosure by the first mortgage holder that threatened my second mortgage. It ended in a half-hour argument between three lawyers on one side (one of them was my own) and me on the other side, and it was finally resolved in my favor. Stubbornness and perseverance paid off for me in that case.

My ventures have not all been profitable. I invested in coal land in Pennsylvania in 1981, but before I could get the coal strip-mined the state legislature enacted tougher environmental laws. Those laws downgraded the value of the coal to the point that it couldn't be used in power plants. After owning the land for 15 years, I finally sold it at a small loss. Sometimes a man can fail because of things beyond his control.

I have changed a few names in this story, especially in the cases of owners and lawyers. Some of the lawyers that I have dealt with were obviously capable and highly intelligent. But with some of the others, their ability and intelligence were not so obvious. I suppose that's the case in every profession.

Laws vary from state to state and are subject to change. Much of this information has cost me dearly, and it is as accurate as I can make it. But no one should rely on the legal or tax information of this book without verifying it with a tax expert or legal advisor.

Joseph C. White

Contents

TOP House at 308 Hanlon, Tampa, Florida. This is the first house I ever owned and it was purchased with "no cash down." Becoming a home owner was very important to a "hillbilly from Tenneesee" who saw the Great Depression up close and personal. BOTTOM This is 5908 La Vista Drive, Alexandria, Virginia, that I purchased in 1957 with $800 borrowed from the Federal Credit Union. This purchase allowed me to begin building equity that years later had grown into large rental apartment buildings that allowed me to retire with significant income while still young enough to enjoy it. (photos by Joseph C. White)

From Farming To Real Estate

LESSON 1: Think of ways to make the deal work. Listen to the customer and THINK.

LESSON 2: Give the customer what he wants. You will lose him if you try to force your preferences on him.

LESSON 3: Even though you may represent the seller, be honest with your buyer. Make sure he knows what he is letting himself in for.

LESSON 4: If it feels like you are cheating someone, you probably are.

LESSON 5: Make it as easy as possible for the customer to buy. Don't rigidly follow some rule or practice simply because everyone else does it that way.

LESSON 6: Beware of long-term contracts for deeds. That is a dangerous way to buy property.

LESSON 7: The customer does not always tell you the real reason he does not buy. It may even be a subconscious thing.

My first taste of real-estate dealing was in 1941, when I was in the U.S. Army at Fort Jackson, South Carolina. My grandfather, who was 81 and no longer able to farm, wanted to sell his house, barn, and 30 acres for $600. It was next door to our farm where I grew up in Tennessee.

Dad wrote me about it and I sent him the money, since I had a small savings account. Grandpa still owed a mortgage of $180, and he told Dad later that he expected me to also pay that off. But Dad thought Grandpa was going to pay off the mortgage out of the money I gave him.

I was on maneuvers at the time, and they could not get in touch with me, so Dad told Grandpa to find another buyer for it and I would be satisfied just to get my money back. Grandpa thought that was fair and he sold it to a neighbor for $800 and paid off the mortgage. I would have been willing to pay off the mortgage too, but I did not have enough money at the time.

My brother Quinton and I got out of the service in late 1945, and we worked one year on the farm. We did that to help Dad financially and to collect our readjustment allowance for one year. The government paid discharged veterans $20 a week for one year to help them adjust to civilian life. In our case, they paid us $100 a month each because we were engaging in the business of farming and made no money until harvest time near the end of the year. But that year convinced us we did not want to make farming our life work. Our methods were labor intensive and totally unlike the no-till, mechanized procedures used later.

♠ ♠ ♠ ♠

After we gathered the crops in late 1946, I went to Florida to work in the citrus harvest. In 1947 I met and married my first wife, who is the mother of my three natural children. A few months later, I saw an ad for a real-estate salesman in the help wanted section of a Tampa newspaper. I got the job, but only after I went to a private school and got a license. A father and son named Spear held the school at night in their real-estate office.

The father had a deep voice that sounded as if he had gravel in his throat and was talking from the bottom of a barrel. He announced that the school would last two weeks, with classes five nights a week for two hours a night. Within that time, he solemnly assured us, "We will teach you everything there is to know about the real-estate business." Before the first evening was over, I remembered the kidding I got when I was a flying instructor in the Army Air Corps: "Them that can, do; them that can't, teach." I suspected the Spears were not doing well in the real-estate business and were running this school to help pay expenses.

The course was primarily a list of questions and answers from previous license examinations for salesmen. This list also included questions and answers from examinations for brokers. I did not stay for all 10 lessons, because they didn't have much to offer except the list of questions and answers. I studied them and passed the test the first time I took it. Then I took the broker's examination and passed it on the first try. There was no requirement for qualifying experience as a salesman. It was easy in Florida in those days, but it got harder in later years.

♠ ♠ ♠ ♠

My first broker was a Pennsylvania Dutchman (his description of himself) named B.H.G. Kistner. He had married his wife about 10 years previously, when they both were in their 60's. They lived in a cottage on a small lake some five miles from the office. He always had a garden, and he worked in it after dark using a battery-powered light strapped to his forehead.

They also kept chickens, and Mrs. Kistner came to the office once a week and brought eggs. She went up one side of the aisle and down the other trying to sell eggs to the sales people and secretaries. She had a 20-year-old car and was proud of the fact that it qualified for antique license plates. Her name was Virginia, but she always signed her name Virginia Giddens Kistner. The Giddens family had been prominent in Tampa society and she wanted everybody to know she was a member of that family. I believe it was her first marriage.

Mr. Kistner either had several identical brown suits or wore the same one most of the time. He wore striped tan shirts and I think he changed them every three or four days. I did not know any better, so I usually wore white shirts to work. He asked me once how I managed to keep my shirts so white. I told him I wore them once and then sent them to the laundry (my wife was working full time also). He gave me a sly little smile and said he wore colored shirts and wore them more than one day. I tried to look surprised.

Mr. Kistner was the broker, but on occasion he ran an ad for himself and showed houses to the people who answered the ad. He liked to argue, and his favorite expression was "oooOOH No! You are WRONG!" I often thought he would rather win an argument than make a sale.

He once showed a customer a house built of stucco on hollow tile (baked tile building blocks, hollow in the middle.) Stucco was like plaster, except it was on the outside of the house. The customer said he liked the house but wanted one built of stucco on metal lath, which was similar to chicken wire. A house built of stucco on metal lath was inferior to a house built of stucco on hollow tile and normally sold for 10 or 15 percent less. That was a common method of home construction in the 1920s and the 1930s, so plenty of them were available.

Mr. Kistner told the customer that the hollow-tile house was stronger and worth more money than a similar house built on metal lath. The customer did not believe him and insisted that a metal lath house was better. Instead of finding him a metal-lath house and making a sale, Mr. Kistner argued with him about it until the customer got angry and walked away. He soon found another agent who sold him what he wanted. He bought a house that Mr. Kistner had among his listings and could have sold to him.

Each salesman selected the property he wanted to advertise and wrote the ads, and Mr. Kistner edited and usually condensed them. He encouraged me to advertise the least expensive house we had listed, especially if it had a low down payment. I sold some junky houses, but they didn't look so bad to me after what I had lived in most of my life on the farm in Tennessee.

I sometimes advertised a house for $2,995. with $500 down, and got 10 or 15 calls a day. I worked from early morning until after dark most days, Saturday included. I averaged about $100 a week in sales commissions. That was considered good, because in those days (1948) the starting salary for a new lawyer was $150 a month and a beginning copilot with an airline was paid that same amount.

♠ ♠ ♠ ♠

A building contractor that we called "Old Man Wills" built the shoddiest new houses I ever saw. He was about five feet three and weighed maybe 110 pounds. He had thin gray hair and pale blue eyes. His lower lip drooped slightly, he slurred most of his words, and a small amount of saliva usually drooled from his mouth. He must have been well into his 80's and his hands shook so much he had to press the heel of his right hand against the top of the desk to sign his name. We had to admire his tenacity to still be working.

He paid low wages and hired workers with marginal skills, and he sold his houses for low prices because they were not worth much. Even so, he sold them on contracts for deed, at 6 percent interest, which provided the easiest terms available. He took low down payments, but he did not give the buyer a deed until the purchase price was paid in full. He sold the contracts at big discounts to two spinster sisters. He built only two or three houses a year, and the sisters bought all his contracts. They then owned the right to all the payments and held the deeds to the properties until the buyer made all the payments over a period of years.

They call these instruments land contracts in some northern states, and they call them installment sales in Pennsylvania. But IRS has a different definition of an installment sale, which can include any sale with payments in different years. Mr. Wills sold the houses for more than they were worth because the down payment was so low and the terms so easy. The seller, or whoever bought the contract, could even put a new mortgage on the property during the term of the contract. They might still owe money on it after the buyer had paid for it in full. The real value of the house was what the sisters paid Wills for the contract, not the inflated price that the buyer promised on the contract for deed. If the buyer ever ran into difficulty and had to sell, he would have a problem, because for the first several years he would owe more on the contract than the house would be worth.

I sold only one Wills house. I was in the office after dark one evening when a man came in and said he wanted to buy a house that night. It had to be a vacant house so he could move in right away. The only such house we had was a Wills house, but the electricity was not on. The customer had a flashlight with him and wanted to go see it anyway. After examining the house by flashlight he insisted on writing a contract. He refused my suggestion that he wait until after daylight and look at it again.

The buyer closed the deal and moved into the house, but I told Mr. Kistner I didn't like the financing arrangements. He brushed aside my concerns, even though he considered himself scrupulously honest. He never explained to any buyer the problems that could arise over the term of the contract, and he did not like it when I questioned the soundness of such an arrangement. I had visions of being sued by some irate buyer when he realized what a mess I had created for him. Call me a coward, but I never showed another Wills house.

A contract for deed can be a useful device if there is a provision that a deed will be delivered and recorded and a mortgage executed as soon as the buyer builds enough equity for a normal down payment. But I would never buy with such a long-term contract for deed unless there was no other way to put a roof over my head. Even then, I would insist that the contract for deed be notarized and recorded at the time of sale.

Some think they reduce the risk by having the deed executed and held in escrow by a title company. But that is not much protection because, at least in Florida, a deed must be delivered to the buyer before the seller dies or else the deed is not valid.

♠ ♠ ♠ ♠

I had another conflict of conscience about that time. I attended a Dale Carnegie course in public speaking, and one of the textbooks for the course was his book *How to Win Friends and Influence People*. I recommend it highly, especially to those who sell for a living.

Several prominent local people were in the class. One was John, the owner of a big hotel on Bayshore Drive. He had raised campaign funds for Fuller Warren, the recently elected Governor of Florida. Warren had campaigned against imposing a sales tax in Florida and had promised to veto such a bill if the legislature should pass one. Many thought that his promise was a major factor in his election. The legislature did pass a sales tax law after his election, and he signed it. He was defeated when he ran for re-election four years later, and most thought it was because he signed the sales tax law after promising he would veto it.

John knew I was in real estate from our discussions in the class, and he called me at work one day and asked me to come to his office to discuss a business proposition. He said his political connections would enable him to learn in advance where new roads and highways would be built. Thus, he could buy rural land along these routes for low prices and could resell for a profit after they announced the locations of the new highways. There would be even bigger profits if he waited to sell until they built the roads.

He wanted me to be his agent and find parcels he could buy along the planned roads. He wanted large tracts that would offer the best chance for future profits, but said these plans would have to be a closely guarded secret. I would also be the listing agent when he was ready to sell. He had access to enough money to buy all the land I could find.

I told him this was a dream opportunity for any real-estate agent, and even more so for someone new to the business. I appreciated the offer, but I did not like the secrecy involved. I told him I grew up on a farm, and if someone had used the same scheme on my family, we would have been furious. I asked him to engage someone else, since there no doubt were other agents in Tampa who would jump at the chance. He said he had someone else in mind also, but I was his first choice. He asked me to think it over and said he would call me again. If he had just asked me to arrange for him to buy certain parcels without telling me why, I would not have had a problem. I did not know enough to say it would have been wrong, but it did not feel right to me. In today's terms, it would be like insider trading in the stock market, and that is illegal.

When he called again I told him I could not do it. He thanked me anyway for meeting with him. I never told anyone about this offer except my wife, and she agreed I had made the right decision. I never knew whether John acted on his plan, or whether he discussed it with anyone else.

♠ ♠ ♠ ♠

Compared to the multiple forms, disclosures, and mountains of paperwork required nowadays for each sale, we had stone-age procedures in 1948 in Florida. The seller under contract paid an abstract company to bring the abstract of title up to date and certify that it contained the complete chain of title for that property. Then the purchaser under contract paid a lawyer to read the abstract and write an opinion of title saying the title was, or was not "merchantable." The abstract company then usually held the abstract in their storage facilities until the next sale of that property. If no abstract existed, or if it could not be found, the seller had the option of paying for a title insurance policy for the buyer instead of building an abstract from scratch.

The settlement was usually held in the office of the real estate broker who computed all the prorations, typed up the deed on approved forms, witnessed and notarized the signatures, and took the deed and mortgage to the court house and recorded them. If the seller was taking back a mortgage, the broker prepared that also. But if there was a new mortgage from a bank, the lending institution prepared the mortgage and gave it to the broker to have executed and notarized.

Mr. Kistner usually recommended one of two lawyers, a Mr. Schonbrun or a Mr. Shaw. They would render an opinion within two or three days and they each had a standard fee of $35. Either of them would then give Mr. Kistner legal advice for free, so long as they didn't have to do any further research.

We did not have a multiple listing service in those days, and we rarely had exclusive listings. Sometimes three or four brokers were working on a property at the same time. At Mr. Kistner's office we had a blackboard on a back wall, out of sight of any customers. When an agent got a written offer on a property, he wrote the property address on the board under the column for sales. There was another column for listings. Once you wrote the entry under sales, no other agent in the office could present an offer on that property without letting you present your offer also.

♠ ♠ ♠ ♠

One Sunday I showed a man a house listed for $2,995 with a $500 down payment, and the seller would hold a mortgage for the balance. It was a two-bedroom frame house built of unpainted cypress boards. The man liked the house and wanted to buy it, but said he could not get the money until 9:00 a.m. Monday morning when his bank opened. It was in a savings account and he could not write a check. He had only one dollar in his pockets, so I took that for a deposit and wrote a contract requiring him to bring in $499 more by 10:00 a.m. Monday morning.

I wrote the sale on the board and called the owner to make an appointment to present the offer at noon the next day.

Mr. Kistner did not like the one dollar deposit. Some of the other agents gave me the horselaugh and said they would never take such a small deposit. But if the $500 had been in a checking account, he would have written me a check for the entire amount. As it was, he gave me all he could raise at the time and agreed to bring in the balance as soon as the bank opened the next day.

About 20 minutes after nine Monday morning, the customer walked in with $499 in cash and the sale went through without a hitch. That one dollar deposit made it a binding contract and the man went to sleep that night knowing he had bought a house. Nobody likes to lose even a dollar, and it is possible that he would not have come in had he not felt obligated. Also, I might have been delayed on my way to work and might not have been in the office when he came in with the money. Some other agent might have written the contract and claimed the commission, or at least a share of it. Normally I would not take a one dollar deposit either, but it is ridiculous to follow a rule blindly when unusual circumstances dictate otherwise

♣ ♣ ♣ ♣

A few weeks later, two brothers from Indiana were looking for a small farm. We found a 10 acre place they liked south of Tampa, but they said they had to go back to Indiana and settle some business before they could sign a contract. They were going to write me when they were ready, and I was to send them a contract to sign. I believed they were serious, so I suggested we go ahead and write the contract and they take all the unsigned copies back with them. Then, when they were ready, they could simply sign and date three copies of the contract, include a deposit check, and mail them back to my broker in the stamped and self-addressed envelope I provided.

I knew it would take about a week for them to get their letter to me and my letter with the contract back to them. That would be one more week they would have to think about it, and I did not want them to have that much time to change their minds. I have had people decide to buy and then change their minds before we could get back to the office to write a contract.

While I was filling in the contract form (hunt-and-peck typing) in the office, Mr. Kistner came by, all smiles. When he learned what I was doing, he wanted to know why I bothered to write the contract if they were not ready to sign it. I explained I was trying to make it as easy as possible for them to buy. He said I was wasting my time. Perhaps he was worried about the few pennies the blank contract forms cost him. But some two weeks later, he came out of his office happily waving the signed contract and deposit check that had just arrived in the mail.

♠ ♠ ♠ ♠

For a year and a half, I never sold a house for more than $8,000. Then I met a couple named Harper who wanted a better house, and we were having trouble finding anything they liked. He made a good salary as a meat cutter and had $1,000 for a down payment. They said they had found the perfect house but could not buy it because the owner wanted $4,000 dollars down. The agent had said the owner would not consider taking their house trailer as a down payment.

We went to look at the house. It was new, it had three bedrooms and two baths, it was built of concrete blocks covered with stucco, and it had a cement tile roof. The Harpers said the owner wanted $13,200 with $4,000 down, and the owner would hold the mortgage. Two real-estate companies had signs on the lot, so I knew it could not be an exclusive listing.

Mr. Harper said the house was open during the day, so they had walked through it and called the agent from one of the signs. He never saw the agent but had talked to him on the phone two or three times. The agent finally had told him not to bother calling again until after he sold his trailer. Mr. Harper said he did not want to sell his house trailer until he knew he could get the house, and he could not buy the house until he sold his trailer.

He told me he was certain he could sell the trailer for $4,000 and he could do it within a month at most. They really wanted the house, and I asked if he would be willing to risk losing the deposit if he failed to sell his trailer within two months. He said yes. So I took them back to their trailer and asked them to wait there for me for a couple of hours.

I consulted the public records and learned that a Mr. Muto owned the house, and I got his address and the legal description of the property. I then went back to the Harpers and wrote a contract for the full price, with a $1,000 deposit and another $3,000 to be paid at closing, which was to be within 60 days. When I presented the offer, I told Mr. Muto the buyer might need 60 days to close because he had to sell his house trailer, but he was willing to forfeit the $1,000 deposit if he failed to raise the rest of the money. Mr. Muto was happy to sign the contract.

When I got back to the Harpers with the signed contract, they were laughing. She had remembered that her father had given her a paid-up life insurance policy as a wedding present, and it had a cash value of $3,900. She did not have to cash the policy, however, because they sold their trailer and we closed the sale on their new house in a little over a month.

A few days later, an angry real estate agent called me and accused me of stealing his customer. He admitted he had talked to Mr. Harper only on the telephone and had never seen him. He had sold the house to the Harpers, he said, and was just waiting for them to sell their trailer. When I explained that Harper did not sell the trailer until three weeks after he signed the contract, he said that was impossible, because Harper had only $1,000 and couldn't contract for the house until he raised another $3,000.

I told him I had no specialized training in either real estate or in selling, and I was so slow I had spent nine years in the third grade. Therefore, if I could find a way for Mr. Harper to make a contract before he sold his trailer, it couldn't be too complicated. He slammed the phone down and never called me again. "Use your head," Dad used to say, "for something besides a hat rack."

♠ ♠ ♠ ♠

Later, another agent told me a story about a man and wife who looked at a house that was just what they had said they wanted. As the agent took them through the different rooms, the wife was excited and he was sure he was going to make a sale. But as they went through the family room, her attitude suddenly changed and she started finding fault with almost everything. "Let's go," she finally said. "I don't want this house." As they went back through the family room on the way out, the agent saw why she did not like the house. About 20 feet from the window in the next-door neighbor's back yard was a shapely young woman in a bikini swimsuit sunning herself by her swimming pool.

(l-r) Oland Bruce White, T.C. White, and Joseph C. White about 1978. My brother Bruce and my Uncle T.C. are now both deceased. Bruce is survived by wife Kristin and two sons, Eric and Steven. (photo courtesy of Joseph C. White)

Double Duty Work

About this time, I started target shooting with a pistol. I had learned to use guns on the farm, and I was doing well for a beginner. Soon, a member of the Tampa Police Pistol Team asked me to join the police force in Tampa, so I could shoot with their team. I finally agreed, and planned to continue to sell real estate in my spare time. I worked that way for six months, but finally gave it up to go back to real estate full time.

During my shifts with the police, I worked in a car assigned to the control of traffic and the investigation of accidents. As the junior officer, I had no say about where we ate lunch. Most of the officers liked to eat at the Rialto Grill, owned and operated by J. Ed Drake and his family. He was short and pudgy and in his mid-50's. His face was wide and flat, he had pale blue eyes, and he combed his thin gray hair over a bald spot. He was friendly and talkative and everyone liked him. He said he had been an FBI Agent in the past, although some said he had been a minor employee of the bureau. He did not like John Edgar Hoover, and he claimed Hoover got to be the Director of the FBI only through the influence of his lover, Evelyn Walsh McLean.

Ed's wife was a likable woman—pretty but not beautiful, and well fed but not obese. She took an active role in his business affairs, and she seemed to be more conservative than he was.

The Rialto Grill charged half-price for meals to any police officer in uniform. Their son worked as a cook in the kitchen, and the cashier was Drake, his wife, or their daughter Betty. They turned an officer's ticket upside down, stuck it on a spindle, and deducted 50 percent from the bill. This did not seem quite right, but I went along with it. It was either do that, do without lunch, or embarrass everybody involved by insisting on paying full price. Later, I heard Drake was running a dice game in the back room, but I never knew that for sure. Tampa had a reputation for being wide open in those days.

Tampa had an automobile racetrack, and Betty Drake married a racecar driver named Frank Luptow. Her father financed a new racing car for him, complete with an Offenhauser engine. This was the best engine available at the time, and Luptow won most of the races he entered. A year or two later, he died from an accident in a stock-car race.

I'm sure Betty had no trouble when she was ready to marry again. She was so beautiful, some speculated she must have been adopted. When she ran the cash register, some of the police officers enjoyed paying the money to her as much as eating for half-price.

♠ ♠ ♠ ♠

When Mr. Drake learned I was selling real estate, he told me he wanted to buy an orange grove. I had listed a 10-acre grove with a small two-acre lake. The lake was an asset because the owners pumped water out of it to irrigate the grove. The owner wanted to sell it, but his wife did not. He finally persuaded her, and they sold it to Drake for $6,500. The trees were young and that was all that it was worth. After the contract was signed by both buyer and seller, Mr. Drake asked me to take his copy to his lawyer.

When the lawyer saw it, he complained that Mr. Drake should have shown him the proposed contract before he signed it. I pointed out that it was the official contract form approved by the lawyers for the Real Estate Board of Tampa.

"Yes," he replied, "but how do I know this property is worth the price?"

I'm sure he knew much more about the law than Mr. Drake did, but I am equally sure Mr. Drake knew more about orange grove values than the lawyer. A real-estate agent occasionally loses a sale, and a buyer passes up a good opportunity, because a lawyer, a relative, or a friend offers financial advice when it is neither asked for nor wanted. I was lucky that the contract was already ratified.

In his excellent book that I will refer to later, Milt Tanzer tells about a customer who was ready to buy a commercial building but first wanted to consult his lawyer.

> "Mr. Raymond spent a couple of days with me looking for an industrial building that was leased to a stable company. We located a $300,000 building for sale that was leased to a computer manufacturer. It had everything he wanted. We drew up a contract and had a verbal agreement with the seller. At the last minute, Mr. Raymond had second thoughts. 'Let me call my attorney,' he said. His attorney, in a 60-second conversation, without knowledge of the proposed investment, advised him against any real estate investment in our 'unstable' economy. 'That's it', Mr. Raymond said, closing up his briefcase. He did not buy. Within two years, the computer company had to expand into an additional building. Mr. Raymond had passed up a long-term, sound real estate investment." *(Real Estate Investments and How to Make Them*, Milt Tanzer, Page 148)

About a year-and-a-half later, Mr. Drake decided the grove was too small for commercial purposes so he asked me to sell it. He priced it at $8,000, which included a 10 percent sales commission. I put an ad in the paper, and got a call the first day. A young girl's voice said, "Mr. White, my mama wants to know if that is the same grove Mr. Drake bought from us before my daddy died." I told her it was the same, and she thanked me and hung up the phone. A few minutes later she called back. "Mr. White," she said, "my mama says to write up the contract and take it to lawyer so-and-so at thus-and-such address. She wants to buy it back."

I took the contract to the lawyer and he read it. He then gave me a handwritten note for her. "This contract looks fine," he wrote, "and Kistner Realty is a reputable broker. However, you are to be the sole judge of the value of the property and the wisdom of this investment. It is not my place to volunteer advice on such matters."

I took her the note, she signed the contract, and the sale closed without incident. I believe that is how a real-estate lawyer should function. That woman obviously had an emotional attachment to that little grove and wanted it back. And she no doubt knew more about its value than the lawyer did.

Soon thereafter, I heard about a 35-acre grove near Tampa that was for sale for $35,000. Mr. Drake knew the grove and wanted to buy it immediately, but the listing broker would not cooperate. He said he had given one of his customers five days to make up his mind and if he didn't take it, he had given another customer five days after that to make up <u>his</u> mind. He sold it the next week to Colin English, the Superintendent of Education for Florida.

A month or two later, a 50-acre grove became available; it had several thousand boxes of ripe oranges on the trees. A seller usually liked to sell a grove with a full crop of fruit, because it would bring a lot more money; and he could pay capital gains taxes on the entire profit, instead of much higher ordinary income taxes on the sale of the fruit. (At that time IRS taxed only 40 percent of long-term capital gains.) The trees were fully grown, and the seller wanted $60,000 including the fruit crop. Mr. Drake did not want to pay more than $1,000 an acre, so they were $10,000 apart on the sale.

Mr. Drake called me one day and said he was ready to pay the asking price for the grove. He said there had been a hard freeze in California the day before, and most of the orange crop had been ruined. He expected the price of oranges to double within a week, and he wanted to buy right now.

I called the owner to make an appointment to present a contract. He said he would be glad to meet with me, but he wanted me to know the price was now $85,000. "But you told me $60,000." I protested. "Nice try, kid," he responded, "but I heard about the California freeze too."

♠ ♠ ♠ ♠

Soon after World War II ended, a man named Gabe Ayala formed a corporation in Tampa to build low-cost homes for veterans. They were selling as fast as he could build them, and he accumulated a great deal of cash in his corporate account. He used the corporation ownership to limit his liability in case the project failed or in case someone sued him.

The corporation had to pay taxes on the corporation profit, and the stockholders then paid taxes on the dividends distributed. The IRS wanted the after-tax profits distributed to the stockholders so they would have to pay personal income taxes on the dividends. Probably to encourage those distributions, they imposed a penalty on any excessive buildup of cash in the corporate account. Since Ayala was the principal stockholder and was reluctant to pay taxes again on all that money, he looked around for some place for the corporation to invest the excess cash.

It was then December and the tax year was about to end, so he had his corporation pay cash for a 40-acre orange grove loaded with ripe fruit. My friend Charley Hayes told me about that deal. That purchase reduced the excess cash in the corporate account so there was no penalty tax. Ayala planned to harvest and sell the oranges in the following tax year, which would give him several months before the problem arose again. In January the California freeze came, the price of oranges went way up, and he sold the orange crop for as much money as he had paid for the entire grove. There is an old saying: "Them that has, gets."

♠ ♠ ♠ ♠

Mr. Drake and Colonel (his first name, not his title) Phelps bought a 40-acre field next to the town limits of Temple Terrace, a suburb of Tampa, and planted it in Texas Ruby grapefruit trees. Mr. Drake told me they paid $1,600 for the land, or $40 an acre. They paid more than the usual price for grove land, because it was a close-in location and it was already cleared. They drilled a well and installed underground water lines from the well to irrigate the rows of trees. They did that in 1950, and after 30 years of producing fancy grapefruit, the land was probably worth a million dollars as building sites for homes.

Buying Our First Home

After our wedding in 1947, my wife and I spent the weekend in Bradenton, about an hour south of Tampa, and came back to work Monday morning. We rented a furnished cabin in the back yard of a house in Seminole Heights. We had to light the gas water heater when we wanted hot water and turn it off when we had all we needed, because it had no thermostat to keep it from overheating. One morning I forgot to turn it off and it stayed on several hours. When I came back the place was full of steam and we were lucky it didn't explode.

We lived there a few months and then rented a furnished, two-bedroom apartment in a pleasant, close-in area. It was in a four-unit building that the owner wanted to sell. Tampa had rent control then, and our rent was limited to $40.25 a month. The owner said it was so low he even took the quarter. He rented it to us because I was in the real-estate business and he hoped I would be better able to sell it if I lived there. It was a good thought, but it didn't work. I didn't sell it, and neither did anyone else while we lived there.

♣ ♣ ♣ ♣

In 1950 a man came into the office and wanted to sell a new house he had just built. It was at 308 Hanlon Street in Tampa, just south of the Hillsboro River and near the water tower of Purity Springs, then the biggest seller of bottled spring water in Tampa. It had two bedrooms, a living room, a kitchen, and a bath. It was a wood-frame house with a kerosene-burning space heater. There was no stove or refrigerator. He wanted $4,995, and he had an FHA appraisal for that amount. He agreed to pay the closing costs and a

5 percent sales commission, and said he would take a small second mortgage. It was illegal to place a second mortgage on FHA financing at the time of the sale, but people often did that later.

We bought the house and the seller paid the closing costs. I had to pay a few dollars to an escrow fund for taxes and insurance, but my sales commission was more than that and I was able to pocket a small amount. I gave him a chattel mortgage on my car for the down payment. A month later we gave him a second mortgage on the house for the same amount and he released the chattel mortgage on the car.

We took title on a Friday, and then went to Sears Roebuck and used our credit to buy a refrigerator, a hot plate, a kitchen table with four wooden chairs, and a sofa that converted into a bed. Sears promised delivery for Saturday morning, because we had to be out of the apartment by then. But they did not bring the furniture until Monday, and we had to sleep on the floor two nights.

About a year later, we bought another two-bedroom house at 2503 St. Isabel Street, near Armenia Avenue on the west side of town. It had asbestos-shingle siding over wood frame and a detached two-car garage. There was a solar water heater, a small chicken house in the back, and a beautiful vegetable garden loaded with produce.

A lime tree, a Ponderosa lemon tree, a guava tree, and two or three orange trees all grew on the half-acre lot. The lemons were large, with thin skins, and each one produced an amazing amount of juice. The lime tree was ever-bearing and we could pick ripe limes from it 10 months of the year. The next year, we bought 15 baby chickens and raised them in the chicken house. They were more trouble than they were worth, and we never did it again. We were lucky to find a place nearby where they processed the chickens for a price and delivered them back to us plucked, cleaned, dressed, and ready for the freezer.

We bought the house on St. Isabel Street for $6,200 with a mortgage guaranteed by the Veterans Administration. We paid nothing down and financed the closing costs. Then, we sold the house on Hanlon Street for several hundred dollars more than we paid for it. A merchant-marine sailor and his wife bought it. They assumed the FHA mortgage and the small second mortgage, and we took a third mortgage for most of our profit. One of the other agents said we were stupid for taking a third mortgage, but the buyers paid it off within two years.

My son David and I drove by the place in 1995, so he could see the first house his parents ever bought. I stopped to take some pictures and saw a woman watching me from a window. I knocked on the door to tell her why I was taking pictures, and she asked me if I was Mr. White. She said they were the ones who had bought it from us 45 years previously. They had applied aluminum siding and the place looked as good as new. They had invested for the future with a small down payment in 1950 and had since enjoyed a mortgage-free home for many years.

(top) My stepson, Stephen W. White, with his wife JanLynn. Stephen attended the Corcoran School of Art and Design and the University of Maryland. He is director of marketing and sales for Aronson & Company, a nationally ranked, top-50 accounting and consulting firm headquartered in Rockville, Maryland. JanLynn attended Fordham and Penn State Universities. (bottom) John Joseph White, grandson, with his mother JanLynn. He is wearing a mortarboard because he has just graduated from nursery school. (photos courtesy of Stephen W. White)

Kistner's Real-Estate Office

Kistner Realty & Insurance had its office at 219 East Lafayette Street, later renamed John F. Kennedy Boulevard. Mr. Kistner was quick to remind anyone who called it Kistner Realty that the name was Kistner Realty and INSURANCE. The insurance secretary sat at the first desk on the left, as you entered, and served as the receptionist for the office. The young insurance agent, Ken Mulder, sat at the next desk. They offered fire and windstorm coverage and tried to write a policy on any house the company listed or sold. They also sold death-and-dismemberment insurance coverage that paid various amounts for death, for the loss of one foot, both feet, one hand, both hands, a hand and a foot, or both hands and both feet. I know it was serious business and it shouldn't have been funny, but sometimes I had to leave the room to keep from laughing when Mr. Kistner was standing in the aisle, eagerly explaining the various benefits to a customer as he tried to sell a policy.

♠ ♠ ♠ ♠

Against the left wall and behind the insurance agent sat Mrs. Ford, the bookkeeper, and behind her were two other desks for secretaries. Several cabinets for active files stood in the back corner on that side. In the back room was a unisex bathroom, a large blackboard on the wall, and storage space for supplies and inactive files.

The office was about 20 feet wide and perhaps 50 feet long. It was furnished with sturdy, solid-wood desks that had seen plenty of service but still had several good years in them. The front of the office was glass, with an entrance door in the middle. The glass front was slanted about 30 degrees toward the street, from the top downward to the bottom. This made room for wooden platforms behind the glass (on either side of the door) for display of pictures of houses. The desks for the salesmen were lined up against the wall on the right side looking from front to back.

♠ ♠ ♠ ♠

Chester Strickland sat at the front desk because he had been there longest. He was a moderately successful salesman but he thought everything was overpriced. He had a serious look on his face most of the time. He was short and stocky and had thin gray hair. He wore round eyeglasses with metal rims, and he looked over the top of them when he was not reading. When I got excited about a new listing, he said it wasn't worth the asking price because he remembered when it sold before the war for a lot less. Strickland thought prices would soon go back down to pre-war levels, and many others shared his views.

Sometimes he stood on the sidewalk in front of the office and talked to people who walked by. He often said to a passerby, "gimme something I can sell." He sold a few houses because he had lived in Tampa many years and knew lots of people. But often, he sat at his desk and waited for customers to come to him. His hands were small and he sometimes closed his right hand into a fist, palm down, and hit the top of his desk with it as he sat staring out into the street. He kept his elbow on the desktop and swung his forearm up and down as he hit the desk gently but firmly. He rapped the desk at three or four second intervals and he usually hit it five or six times before he stopped. Each time he hit the desk he left his forearm flat on the surface until he was ready to rap again. Then he raised his forearm until his fist was a few inches off the desk and rapped the desk again. Sometimes he continued for 10 or 12 raps, while staring out the front window with a far-away look, as if in deep thought. He may not have realized he was doing it.

I seldom saw Strickland spend any money. He didn't go to lunch, he didn't smoke, he didn't drink soft drinks, he didn't chew gum, and he didn't eat candy bars or other snacks. Years later I watched a golf match on television and listened to Dave Marr commenting. Orville Moody was playing, and Marr said Moody was the most frugal player on the tour. The other announcer replied that Moody had recently won $150,000 in a tournament. "That's a lot of money to take out of circulation," Marr said softly, as if to himself. When I heard that, I thought of Chester Strickland.

At the second desk was Charles A. Hayes, a young Lt. Colonel in the Air Force Reserves. He was tall and wiry and wore little round eyeglasses. Charley was friendly and loved to talk. His words seemed to come from the bottom of his throat, and his voice was deeper and more resonant than average. Mr. Strickland claimed he had heard Charley talk a customer into a sale and keep talking until he talked him out of it. Nevertheless, he worked hard and he was the top salesman in the office. His wife was the only child of the owner of an orange grove on Lake Magdaline, near Tampa. Her name was Isobel and she was an announcer at a local radio station. She called Charley "Bosco" because he was so fond of a chocolate-flavored drink by that name. They had no children.

Charley wanted to buy an orange grove, and one of his neighbors decided to sell a prime 25 acre grove for $25,000, including a crop of fruit. It was close to Tampa and had mature Temple orange trees and four or five hundred feet of frontage on a big clear lake. Charley immediately consulted his banker about the financing, but he was one day too late; someone else bought it. In later years that property became extremely valuable as building sites for homes with close-in lake frontage.

♠ ♠ ♠ ♠

My desk was behind Hayes, and behind me was Clarence Stevens, who had moved recently from Detroit. Clarence was fairly short and stocky, and had a smug, I-know-more-than-you-know look. He was fond of telling everyone how they used to do things in Michigan. I remember watching Stevens as he sat at his desk with his arms folded, contentedly puffing on his pipe and waiting for someone to come in and buy a house from him. If he had spent as much time really working at real estate as he did cleaning, filling, tamping, lighting, and puffing on that pipe, he might have been a success. He never did much business, and that was not surprising because his pipe kept him too busy.

A fine old gentleman named Mr. Douglas sat at a desk near the back of the office. He was tall and lean, and always wore suits of good quality, even in hot weather. His wife had money, according to reports, and he came into the office primarily to have something to do with his time. He lived in a big house in Bayshore Estates, near the office.

One day he made a sale, and he sat at his desk for a long time, smoking an expensive cigar and fondling the contract. He unfolded it and then refolded it. Then he opened it, re-read it, and folded it again. He pressed the folds between his thumb and forefinger and pulled the folds through them, as if to make the folds sharper. He was like a kitten with a toy. He seemed to be in deep thought and may not have realized what he was doing with his hands. I have no doubt he was highly intelligent and he could have done more business if he had wanted to work harder. I think Mr. Kistner allowed him to stay on because he was an old friend.

At one of the desks farther back was Michael Credno, who had been a professional musician. He had some strange ideas, such as putting exactly one dollar's worth of gas in his car each morning on the way to the office. Nobody talked much to Mike, because he didn't stop talking long enough to allow it. He never did much business while I was there. He could talk endlessly about a restaurant his brother owned and about his days as a musician and all the girls who used to hang around the band. Mike had black hair, dark eyes, and full lips. He was married but he had an eye for the ladies.

Jean Kooy (rhymes with gooey) was one of the secretaries in the office. She was tall and slender, attractive but not beautiful, and single. After I left to join the Border Patrol, I had occasion once to come back to Tampa and visit the old Kistner office. Jean cornered me and kept talking about Mike "CREGno," as she called him. She was pressing me to tell her if I thought Mike was a nice guy. It was obvious that she had more than a passing interest in him.

Clinton Ainsley occupied the next desk. He was young, had a new license, and was obsessed with the idea of having his money work for him. He was short and moderately portly, and he walked with his toes pointing slightly inward, as a pigeon does. He slicked his hair down and combed it straight back. He spoke with a low, soft voice that was almost a moan. Sometimes I had to strain to hear him clearly. He didn't make many sales. Perhaps he did better after he gained more experience.

Mr. Smith sat at the next desk. He was a hard worker and fast talker, and he worked mostly on land and commercial lots. He radiated excitement most of the time and always seemed to be in a hurry. He wore casual clothes that did not always match, but perhaps he dressed that way because he spent a lot of time tramping around on acreage and vacant lots.

Mr. Smith listed five 10-acre tracts on North Florida Avenue. The owner had subdivided 50 acres into tracts 330 feet wide and deep enough to make 10 acres, about 1,300 feet. "Going back all the way to the proposed Central Avenue," he said in his ads. They were priced at $2,995 each, with 10 percent down, just enough to pay the sales commission (for land), and the owner would hold the mortgage for 10 years.

I don't recall how many of them Mr. Smith sold. I do remember he was fortyish, was bald except for a fringe around the sides, had a roundish head like Charley Brown in the Peanuts comic strip, and pronounced acres as "akuhs."

Mr. Sol Rivlin occupied the last desk. He did not have a real estate license, so he was not allowed to sell houses. He worked only on business opportunities such as liquor stores and delicatessen stores. If the deal involved a new or revised lease, he had to get Mr. Kistner to negotiate that. He was bald in front and swarthy, and his face usually glistened as if he had just rubbed suntan oil on it. He was not much more than five feet tall and not much less than four feet wide. He wore bright-colored shirts and multi-colored ties that didn't always harmonize with the shirts.

Mr. Rivlin didn't own a car, and he may not have known how to drive, since he had previously lived in New York City most of his life. He either persuaded his customers to pick him up in their cars or he hired a taxi. He frequently had a cigar in his mouth, although sometimes he did not light it and just chewed on it. He had a deep, booming voice that carried all the way to the front of the office. He did very little business and stayed only a few months.

Rivlin was about as different from Mr. Kistner as anybody could be. I could never understand why the boss hired him, unless he thought that was what it took to sell business opportunities. If the Olympic Committee had scheduled an event for aggressiveness, Mr. Rivlin would have had a good chance to win a medal.

♠ ♠ ♠ ♠

Mr. Kistner never hired female sales agents. Some said his wife wouldn't allow it, but that may not have been the only reason. He no doubt lost business because of that policy, because some of the most successful agents are women. A few other agents came and went during the time I was there, but I cannot remember all of them. One of them, Ralph Peters, left to work in an AAA auto club office in Ocala, Florida.

♠ ♠ ♠ ♠

One day a man came in who wanted to sell 40 acres at Land-o-Lakes, a community a few miles North of Tampa. Several of us went with him to look at it. He had just cut the timber, and pine tops were spread around on the land. He wanted $40 an acre, for a total of $1,600, and he would pay a 10 percent commission. He wanted just enough down to pay the sales costs, and he would hold the mortgage for 10 years at 6 percent interest, the prevailing rate at the time.

We agents agreed there was no chance he could get that price and we didn't even bother to write an open listing on it. Thirty years later, that 40 acres was part of a highly desirable community of high-priced homes.

The Robinson and White cousins, about 1925. Front row (l-r) Eunice White, Quinton White, and Lucy Jane Robinson. Back row (l-r) Eugene Robinson, Charlie Robinson, Joseph C. White, and Noah Robinson. Eugene Robinson and two of his sons now own more than 2,000 acres of super-rich farm land in Louisianna. (photo courtesy of Joseph C. White)

A Local Building Boom

LESSON 8: If you invest in a franchise, don't forget to consider a covenant not to compete. Remember what Lumberville did to Brown-Mason.

Charley Hayes eventually left Kistner Realty to handle the sales for Brown-Mason, Inc., a new construction company that built low-cost homes financed by loans insured by the Federal Housing Authority. Brown was trained as an architect, and both Brown and Mason had worked for the FHA until they resigned to get in on the building boom. They built small frame houses with two bedrooms, a living room, a kitchen, a bath, and a carport for $6,295, with $445 down, including the lot. Each house contained 720 square feet of floor space and was built on a poured concrete slab. They had a dozen or more under construction at a time, and they finished two a week, and sometimes three.

Charley Brown and Charley Mason were the partners. Brown was smaller than average, standing about five feet five inches tall and weighing probably 140 pounds. His wife, Gwen, was even smaller than he was. Charley Brown's father was an old-timer who had been a builder for many years and still built a house now and then. I think he used to do much of the manual labor himself, but his son never did.

"I don't see how them boys can call theirselfs builders," the father said to me one day, "when they ain't ever dug out a tree stump in their lifes." Anyone who has never had to dig out a tree stump could never appreciate what a big job it is. Nowadays if a builder has a big tree stump right where he has to put a house, he just calls someone with a gasoline-powered stump grinder and has him come and chew up the stump.

The bookkeeper/accountant for the company was Al Wilson, and he wrote the commission checks. He was thirtyish, somewhat shy, and single. He sometimes had to restrain Charley Mason by telling him the IRS would not go along with some of the schemes he proposed.

The four of them (Brown, Mason, Hayes, and Wilson) formed a joint venture and bought a 700-acre ranch a few miles north of Tampa in Pasco County. I think they were excited by the prospect of having all that land to develop some day. They raised cattle on it for a while, but I left town and never learned how it turned out.

Charley Brown was a licensed private pilot and owned an airplane, a Beechcraft Bonanza. It was a low-wing, high-performance plane, with four seats and one engine. Aviation people called it unforgiving, meaning if the pilot made a serious mistake he could crash. On several occasions Charley took his wife, and sometimes another couple, on weekend trips to Havana, Cuba. Havana is only 90 miles from Miami, and it probably was not more than a two or three hours flight from Tampa for the Bonanza. If he ever had any problems flying the plane, I never heard of them.

Charley Mason was four or five inches taller than his partner. He was thin, but he had a little potbelly that looked out-of-place on his beanpole body. Brown was easy going, friendly, and relaxed, but Mason was restless and had a hard time sitting still for long. Even in his quieter moments, he often fidgeted with his car keys or with something on his desk. If he had a wife I never knew it. After they dissolved the partnership a few years later, Brown built houses on his own and Mason was a salesman for an office furniture retailer. I never knew why they broke up the business.

Each partner drove a new Buick—paid for, owned, and maintained by the corporation. Charley Mason drove his to the office one Sunday, parked it outside the door, and left the engine running. He intended to stay only a few minutes, but he got involved with phone calls and was there about three hours. He forgot that his car was still running and the engine overheated and suffered severe damages.

♠ ♠ ♠ ♠

Lumberville, a big lumber company from Miami, gave Brown-Mason a franchise for an outlet across the street from their office. Brown-Mason bought the land and made a substantial investment in the new Lumberville facility. It was highly successful at first; but they neglected to get a covenant not to compete, and the parent company opened its own store within less than a year. It was only two miles from the Brown-Mason Lumberville store and was three times as big. After that, the franchise got very little business except from its owner, Brown-Mason Builders.

One of the employees at the Lumberville franchise was a handsome young man named Otis Millen. One day Charley Mason asked him how much he knew about paint.

"I don't know anything about paint, Mr. Mason," Otis replied. "Nada, zero, zip."

"Well you do now," Mason said. "I'm going to open a paint store, and you are going to be the manager."

They built an addition to the side of the Brown-Mason office and opened the paint store there, with Millen as manager. After that, Brown-Mason builders bought all their paint through that store.

♠ ♠ ♠ ♠

Brown-Mason paid Charley Hayes a specified commission for each house they built, even if the contract was written up in the office when he was not there. In return, he had to find vacant lots to build on, and that was more difficult than selling the houses. He also had to follow up on all the details of the sale and go to the closing to represent the builders. He got no extra money for finding the lots.

He was making plenty of money, although he had little time for himself. He kept trying to get me to join him, but I was reluctant to leave Mr. Kistner because he had been good to me. Charley could have had any one of many agents in the Tampa area, but for some reason he wanted me. He knew I was married and was hungry enough to work hard, and he knew me well enough to trust me.

In mid-1953 Charley finally made an offer I could not refuse. He was taking his wife to Europe for six weeks and he needed someone to run his office while he was away. He offered to make me a permanent, full partner, with everything split 50-50. And while he was in Europe, I would get all the sales commissions on everything sold during that six weeks. We never had anything in writing, not even a handshake to bind the bargain. We both understood the agreement and we trusted each other. I accepted his offer and sold 19 houses during that six weeks. That earned me as much money as I had made in most years previously.

All of Brown-Mason's closings were handled by Sam Gibbons, a young lawyer with the family firm of Gibbons and Gibbons. Sam was later elected to Congress and served there many years. He was on the Ways and Means Committee, and he got to be Chairman for seven months after Mr. Rostenkowski stepped down in May 1994. He lost the chair after the Republicans took over later that year.

I went to Sam's office once when I was working in the central office of the immigration service in the early 1970s. He had frequent contacts with Charley Hayes and me at the Brown Mason closings and he remembered us well. He told me that Hayes usually brought his military uniform to the office and put it on after work to go directly to his reservists drills one night a week. When he came back to the office after drill one night, there was an intruder in the office who stabbed him to death with a knife.

Border Patrol Days

LESSON 9: No lawyer can know everything about the law, and you will know more than your lawyer knows about some things. "When in doubt, check it out" is a good rule.

I grew up with guns on the farm and had been involved in target shooting (pistol) since 1948. Once a month, I competed in an informal local match, and in March of each year I competed in the National Midwinter Matches, which were always held at the Tampa Police pistol range. I also went to the National Pistol Championships in 1952, since they were held that year at Jacksonville, Florida. I got to know the members of the U.S. Immigration Border Patrol Pistol Team, and they urged me to join that organization so I could shoot with their team.

I finished 11th in the individual standings at the National Matches and finished third in 1953 at the Midwinter matches. A job with the federal government sounded good because of the retirement benefits and because the Border Patrol would pay for all my ammunition and would send me to matches at their expense. In addition, my wife had been urging me to find a job where I did not have to work so many hours in the week. I also had the silly notion that I could contract for and build one house a year in my spare time and sell it for a profit to supplement my income. I knew two police officers that had been doing that.

♠ ♠ ♠ ♠

The Border Patrol was hiring only for employment west of the Mississippi River, since most of the jobs were there. For that reason, they scheduled no entrance examinations in the East, so I took the test at Border Patrol headquarters in Washington, D.C. They made this special arrangement because the chief of the Border Patrol was an avid shooter and he wanted me on his pistol team. Harold Barney, an officer of the Tampa Police Department and a member of their pistol team, went with me. We both passed, but he decided not to take the job because he didn't want to move from Tampa. I took the offer from Charley Hayes to sell for Brown-Mason homes and worked there several months until I got the appointment to the Border Patrol.

I entered on duty at the Border Patrol Academy, McAllen, Texas, in October 1953. I brought my wife and two-year-old son with me, along with everything else we could haul in the car. We rented a furnished apartment and left all our old furniture in Tampa to be sold with the house on St. Isabel Street. Our old stuff wasn't worth moving from Florida to Texas, and the government didn't pay moving expenses to the first duty post.

The new job was GS-6 Patrol Inspector Trainee. An automatic promotion to GS-7 would come as soon as I successfully completed a year of probation. The pay would be less than I had been making, but there would be many fringe benefits, including a great retirement plan. Brown-Mason did not pay sales commissions until the houses were built and the sales closed, so I had a substantial amount still coming from my previous sales. In addition, we had the house on St. Isabel Street to sell, and that also helped us over the first couple of years in the Patrol. Charley Hayes sold that house for us after we left.

After the two months' school at McAllen, I was assigned to New Orleans, Louisiana, where we rented a furnished apartment for a year. There was no border to guard at New Orleans, but we kept busy rounding up alien sailors who had deserted and remained in the United States when their ships left the country. We also kept a lookout for illegal aliens traveling from the Mexican border on their way to harvest sugar cane, vegetables, or citrus in Florida.

After a year in New Orleans, I transferred to Miami, Florida, where we bought another house for about $11,000 with the remainder of my VA loan eligibility. The mortgage was still on the Tampa house, but I had used only a small part of my entitlement because the mortgage was so small. The house we bought had three bedrooms and two baths. It was a brick house in North Miami. We were able to get another 100 percent VA loan because I was eligible for a VA guarantee for more than the total of both loans.

In early 1956, after two and a half years in the Border Patrol, I was promoted to Airplane Pilot, GS-11, and transferred to the Southeast Regional Headquarters at Richmond, Virginia. That was a four-grade promotion, which normally was not allowed under the Civil Service rules. But I had been an Air Corps Pilot in World War II, and I was qualified for the position. Since there were no lower grades for pilots, the Department of Justice wrote to the Civil Service Commission asking them to waive the rule in my case. That was commonly known as a "J" letter. They also did this for several other GS-7 Border Patrolmen who had been military pilots.

At Richmond, I used a twin-engine Beechcraft plane (an old military C-45) to fly officials on inspection trips around the 13 states in the Region. After a year, the Immigration Service decided they did not need an airplane there. At about the same time, a pilot vacancy came up in Washington, D.C., and they transferred me there to be the Assistant to the Chief of Air Operations in the National Headquarters. In 1959, the Service transferred the chief to another position, and promoted me to Chief of Air Operations, GS-13. That was an amazing streak of lucky breaks for me, but I did not see fit to look a gift horse in the mouth, so to speak.

♠ ♠ ♠ ♠

Ed Topmiller had been my Sector Chief when we were in New Orleans. After I transferred to Washington, he called me and insisted we call on his sister, who also lived in Washington. She was working for a homebuilder, and she told us about a brick house for sale in Fairfax County. The owner had bought it new from her company and financed it with a 100 percent VA mortgage, which was assumable.

The owner's name was Doswell, and he wanted only $800 for his interest in the house. He needed to sell because he worked for the railroad and was being transferred to another city. He had made some improvements, including a brick barbecue on the back of the lot and a room air conditioner in the living room. I borrowed the down payment with a signature loan from the Federal Credit Union, and bought the house subject to his VA mortgage. That was the seed money that eventually grew into a 30-unit apartment building in Florida and a lifetime of financial independence for me.

When we moved in, we contracted to have a fence installed around the back yard. Jody, our oldest child, was not yet six, and we wanted to keep him in the yard without having to watch him all the time. The woods came up to the back of our lot, the barbecue was right next to the back, and the fence went between the barbecue and the woods. I got the bill for the fence two or three days after it was installed and sat down at the dinette table to write the check. As I opened my checkbook, I looked out the back window and saw Jody go up on the barbecue, over the fence, and into the woods.

David, our second child, was born soon after we moved to that house. Melissa, our youngest and the only girl, was born in 1960 just after I was transferred to San Juan, Puerto Rico as District Director. I went there alone and entered on duty. Then I returned for her birth and went back again after mother and daughter were well enough. I then stayed a few weeks and came back to move the family when Melissa was five weeks old. The Commissioner of Immigration wanted me to do it that way, because he wanted me to enter on duty the day after the previous incumbent left. He said he did not like the incumbent deputy director and wanted to make sure he knew he was not going to get the job. Also, he probably didn't want him to have time to contact any friends in high places and try to bring political pressure to bear on the commissioner. We didn't buy a house in Puerto Rico. We thought the prices were high, and we expected to be there only two years, since that was the service policy at the time.

As it turned out, we stayed in Puerto Rico four years, and I got another promotion when they reclassified the position to GS-14. We rented the house in Virginia to a cousin who made the mortgage payment for his rent. When the cousin moved, we gave the management to the Cafritz Company and this worked well for a time. Then Cafritz Management went bankrupt and we lost three months' rent they owed us. I was told Mr. Cafritz was a multi-millionaire who hid behind his management corporation to avoid personal liability. We finally rented the house to a soldier who worked in data processing at the Pentagon, and he and his wife lived there several years.

♠ ♠ ♠ ♠

In 1964, I transferred from Puerto Rico to Richmond, Virginia, as the Assistant Regional Commissioner, Investigations. I stayed there six years, and during that time we owned four houses. We rented for a month or two and then bought a big house on Zell Lane from an owner who had already bought another house. We soon learned there were 50 kids living within three blocks of us, so then we sold and bought a house on Westham Parkway, with a big lot and many oak trees. It was old and needed work.

After we spent several thousand dollars to renew the furnace and remodel the kitchen, we got nervous about having so much money invested there and we sold for a small profit. We then bought a much less expensive house on Hanford Street that had four bedrooms but no family room. My wife found that house while I was on a business trip.

A year later, I saw an ad for a house on Bexhill Road, about two blocks from us. An FBI agent offered it for sale because he was being transferred. It had a big, paneled family room, and my wife fell in love with it the minute she saw it. I wrote a contract to buy it with a 100 percent loan that was guaranteed by the Veteran's Administration. I had learned that my two previous VA loans had been paid off, and I was able to get my eligibility restored. We did not lose any money on any of these houses.

My banker had recommended an attorney named John Smart who handled the closings on the other houses we had bought and sold. He taught real-estate law at the local college at night, and I thought that proved he knew everything. The other deals were routine, but a problem arose with this one.

The VA required a survey, and it showed a small utility building on the back of the lot that was closer to the lot line than the building code allowed. Mr. Smart said I would have to move the building and then have the property surveyed again. I told him the building was on skids and was not fixed to the ground; perhaps for that reason the VA would waive the apparent violation. He said that was not possible; that I would have to move the building.

I didn't want to wait. According to law at the time, the interest rate on the VA insured mortgage would be the rate established by the VA and in effect on the day of closing, and there were indications the rate would go up soon. Their office was in Roanoke, a three-hour drive from Richmond. I called an official there and he said I could apply for a waiver by submitting pictures to show the building was not fixed to the ground. I took the pictures and drove them to Roanoke. While I was there, they gave me a letter removing the requirement for a new survey.

I then called Mr. Smart, gave him the news, and told him I wanted to close the sale by Friday of that week, which was two days away. He asked why I was in such a hurry. I told him I wanted to get in ahead of a possible rate increase. He said I should not worry, because the most that would happen would be an increase in the discount points the seller would have to pay. At the time the law required the seller to pay those discount points. He reminded me he taught real estate at the college and understood these things.

I told him I was the one at risk, and I wanted it closed no later than Friday. If he would not do it, I would get another lawyer who would. With some complaining, he finally had the settlement Friday afternoon. Early the following Monday morning the VA rate went up, but we got in just under the wire, so to speak. If we had closed on Monday at the higher interest rate, it would have cost the seller less money for the points, but that was his problem, not mine.

This was my first apartment building, located at 706 N. Belmont, Richmond, Va. John Elam, the Realtor® who helped me find it, is shown here some 36 years after the purchase. I bought the building for $30,000 and sold it three years later for $37,000, which was 400 percent net profit on the cash I had invested. (photo by Joseph C. White)

My First Apartment Building

LESSON 10: When you buy income-producing property, use leverage when you reasonably can. It can multiply your profit many times over.

LESSON 11: Do not let the tenants' problems become your problems. "If you have to eat a live frog, eat it quick," I read somewhere. "And if you have to eat two live frogs, eat the big one first."

Richmond had many old apartment houses. After we had been there a couple of years, I started thinking about buying one as an investment for the future. John Elam, a sales agent with Morton Thalhimer Realtors, advertised a six-unit building at 706 North Belmont Street that showed promise, near Monument Avenue. Each unit had two bedrooms, one bath, a front porch, and a small den. The apartments were renting unfurnished. All the leases were for one year and required 90 days written notice before the expiration date, or otherwise they would automatically renew for another year. Across the top of the leases in big, black, block letters was printed "IRONCLAD LEASE."

The building was three stories, all solid brick, and had no elevator. One apartment was vacant and had been renovated, and one was rented to a woman who was in the hospital and not expected to live. I called Tommy Dickson, a man I knew who owned three or four apartment buildings in the area, and he said his units were always full. He rented them furnished by the week, including utilities. He said it was a lot of work, but it paid off.

The owner of this building was being transferred to Rocky Mount, North Carolina, and he was eager to sell it. I had John submit an offer, and I bought it for $30,000 with just enough down to pay the sales commission and the seller's closing costs. I assumed a first mortgage and gave him a second mortgage for the balance.

As soon as the sale closed, I talked to all the tenants except the woman in the hospital, who died within a month or two. One couple took a hard line and demanded that I repaint the apartment and remodel the kitchen or else they would move. I made some notes and said I would get back to them.

I came back the next night with my copy of their lease, which still had several months to go. I had written in the margin with a fountain pen, "By mutual agreement between the parties, this lease is hereby amended to allow either party to cancel this lease by giving the other party 60 days written notice in advance." I told them I had just bought the building and was not prepared to make the improvements they demanded. So I was doing the next best thing; I was changing the lease so if they wanted to move they wouldn't have to wait almost a year for their lease to expire.

I signed my copy of the lease and handed it to them. They looked at each other in surprise, as if they did not know what to do. I then said "That is what you said you want, isn't it?" They said they guessed so and both signed it; and we then made the same changes on their copy and all signed it. The next time their rent payment was due, I gave them 60-days' notice to move. Perhaps that was a sneaky thing to do. But after they made such a fuss about moving out if I didn't meet their demands, I decided to fight fire with fire.

After they were out, I went in with a bucket of soapy water and a big sponge. The walls were just dirty and didn't need paint. Strangely enough, we were still on friendly terms after they moved.

I gave the other tenants notice 90 days before their leases expired. When they were out, I put secondhand furniture in the apartments and rented them by the week. Within a year I rented them all on a week-to-week basis. I had everybody sign a rental agreement that spelled out the rights of the tenant and the landlord. By putting in inexpensive, used furniture and renting by the week, I raised the yearly income to almost double what it had been. The operating profits more than paid for all the improvements and the furniture.

A woman with two young children rented one of the second floor apartments. After a couple of weeks her parents moved in with her, in violation of the written agreement. The father had one wooden leg and the mother was in a wheelchair. About a week later she couldn't pay her rent. The next week she could pay for only one week. Pretty soon she was three weeks behind. The next time rent was due, she told me she was sorry but she couldn't pay any of the back rent, all she had was enough for the current week.

I suggested she use that money to rent another apartment. I said I would make her a gift of the back rent she owed me and would even help her move. She thought that would not be fair, because she owed me for three more weeks and eventually would pay me. I assured her I would rather make her a gift of that rent to help her get back on her feet. She moved out the next day, and I hauled three carloads of her stuff to the new place.

I didn't like the thought of having to bring the sheriff with an eviction notice to put her things out on the street, while her two little kids, her mother in a wheelchair, and her father with one wooden leg stood around looking sad. She thought I was a wonderful person for giving her that free rent, but I was only taking the coward's way out. I was sorry for her, and I wished I had been in a position to help her more. But I had to make the mortgage payments or lose the building, and the bank was not interested in my problems with tenants.

♠ ♠ ♠ ♠

I sold that building after I transferred to Washington, and made a profit of more than four times my initial investment. That illustrates the advantage of leverage in real estate investments. For a simple example:

> Two men buy similar properties for $100,000 each. One pays all cash and the other pays $10,000 down and gets a mortgage for $90,000. Eventually, they sell them for $150,000 each. They each made a $50,000 profit, but which had a greater return on his investment?
>
> The one who paid all cash made a 50 percent return on his $100,000 investment, but the one who invested only $10,000 made the same $50,000 profit, which is 500 percent on his $10,000 investment. That is because when the sale price goes up the mortgage does not.

This is simplified, because there would be some adjustments because of the payments on the mortgage; but this demonstrates the power of leverage.

♠ ♠ ♠ ♠

Pyramiding is the basis for multiplying profits. The money from the sale of a building is invested as a down payment on a much more expensive building. That greatly increases the return on the original investment. That is possible because there are four ways to make money on a rental building:

> A. You normally have a cash flow from the rents you collect from the tenants, after you deduct operating expenses and capital improvements.
>
> B. The monthly payment on your mortgage is for principal and interest, and sometimes for property taxes and insurance. The portion that is principal reduces your mortgage balance and increases your equity in the property. The interest, taxes, and

insurance are expenses of doing business and are deductible for tax purposes.

C. You get an income tax reduction for depreciation that can be deducted from your profits and usually from other ordinary income. If you sell and have to pay capital gains taxes on this depreciation you took, the rate is lower than on ordinary income.

D. Over the long haul, real estate has always appreciated in value, because of inflation, increases in rental income, or other causes.

The reduction in mortgage balance plus the increase in value through appreciation usually combine to give you the profit when you sell. Moving your increased equity into a larger property after a few years increases the benefits from these two factors because of the advantage of leverage.

3004 Monument Avenue, Richmond, Va. Bought in 1966 in a complicated purchase with nothing down, but with all cash to the seller. Converted from 12 units to 18 units and rented furnished by the week. Sold in 1974. Provided cash flow that enhanced our style of living and paid for four years at a university for our oldest child. Net proceeds from sale used for down payment on 30 units in Florida. (photo by Joseph C. White)

Moving Up To A 12-Unit Building

LESSON 12: Make sure your sales contract stipulates what goes with the house. If you expect to get the stove and refrigerator, the draperies, the window-unit air conditioner, the washer and dryer, or the chandelier in the dining room, PUT IT IN THE CONTRACT. I have heard of sellers that even dug up favorite bushes from the yard and took them when they left.

LESSON 13: You cannot be a successful real estate investor and be completely safe all the time. Occasionally you must take calculated risks. Think, analyze, plan, and then act. Remember that a good opportunity usually looks better after it has passed you by than it did when you had your chance.

LESSON 14: A law degree does not make a person an expert on a real estate venture. Question every appraisal that is presented to you. This is not an exact science. Member of the Appraisers Institute (MAI) is the highest designation there is for appraisers, but even they can differ widely in their valuations of the same property. Every appraisal is based on certain assumptions, and changing the assumptions will change the appraised value. Sometimes the assumptions are shaded one way or another to suit the wishes of the person paying for the appraisal. Check with other sources, as many as possible.

LESSON 15: Try to find well-located investment buildings in sound condition that need mostly cosmetic improvements. Do not go overboard on improvements. If the building is an ugly sow's ear, just make it a nice sow's ear. Do not try to make it into a silk purse, because you will tie up so much money in it you may never get it back.

LESSON 16: Don't try to steal every property you buy. If you do, you will miss out on some good deals.

LESSON 17: Unless you buy a fairly large apartment complex, plan to expend plenty of your own time and effort. Learn to do the simple management and maintenance jobs yourself. If you do not, much of your profit will be spent on management costs.

At 3004 Monument Avenue, one block from the first building, was a three-story building with four units on each floor. It was solid brick and showed no outside cracks or mortar problems. It was 50 years old, and the electric wiring had been completely renewed. Seven of the apartments were vacant, and most of them were in such bad condition they could not be rented. The owners lived in another state, and a local real estate broker managed it. Neither the owners nor the management company wanted to spend any money on it. I found out later they once had a general contractor go over it and tell them what it needed. He wanted $50,000 to put it in first-class condition. They thought that was out of the question, so it just sat there. Everybody can have 20/20 hindsight, but they should have asked for an estimate to put it only into good enough condition to rent the apartments profitably. If an apartment is clean and well located, tenants will put up with many shortcomings in return for reasonable rent.

The kitchens had little hang-on sinks with no cabinets, and all the bathrooms had old leg tubs with no showers. (This was before those leg tubs became fashionable as antiques.) All the floors were wooden, including those in the kitchens and baths, and they were badly in need of refinishing. The floors sagged in places, but there were no serious cracks in the walls or ceilings. A tenant in one apartment had painted all the walls black before he moved out. The building had a built-up (flat) roof with minor leaks, and it had a big basement. Steam radiators provided heat from an oil-fired furnace, converted recently from coal. A 1,000 gallon oil tank in the basement could be filled from outside the building. I could buy heating oil at that time for 25 cents a gallon.

There was no elevator. Inside stairs led to the central hallways on each floor, and doors led from the hallways to front porches on each level. The six apartments in the back (two on each level) each had a bedroom, a living room, a kitchen, and a bath, with entrance doors at the end of the hallway. The six apartments in the front were the same, with entrance doors from the side of the hallway into the living room of each apartment. In addition, there was a second bedroom in the front of each of these apartments, each with its own bath and separate entrance from the front porch.

All the kitchens had doors leading to small wrought-iron porches and flights of metal stairs that served as fire escapes. For the front apartments the kitchen porches were on the sides of the building. For the back apartments they were on the back of the building.

All the apartments were being rented unfurnished on yearly leases. The front (two-bedroom, two bath) apartments rented for $10 a month more than the smaller ones in the back. A man had been living for many years in the front bedroom of one of the ground-floor apartments. The rest of that apartment was vacant, and so were six others. At these rents the annual income would have been less than $11,000 a year with full occupancy.

I found this building by looking around the neighborhood and then researching the public land records. It was a likely prospect because it was obviously neglected and the owners lived in another state. Public records usually show the name and address of the person who pays the taxes, but that is not necessarily the owner. Sometimes they send tax bills to a management company and the records don't reveal the name of the owner.

You can call the company, of course, but they normally want a sales commission if you buy it. I was lucky in this case, and I got the names and the addresses of the two owners from the tax records. The building obviously needed better management since 7 of the 12 units were vacant. Yet it was in a great location one block from the bus line, it seemed structurally sound, and many of the problems were cosmetic.

I knew a professional appraiser who worked for the city who agreed to look at it informally for free. I had met him before in connection with land he tried to buy at an auction. He told me three-room furnished apartments near the bus line were renting readily. I already knew that from Tommy Dickson, who quit his job at the Post Office to devote all his time to his rental apartments.

This appraiser said it had potential, but in no case should I pay more than $40,000 for it, and I should buy it for less if possible. "It is not a nice property," he explained.

Two sisters had inherited it when their mother died a couple of years earlier, and their husbands took a hard-line attitude about the price. I went to my lawyer, Mr. Smart, and asked him to write an offer for $40,000, contingent on financing and a couple of other things. He protested because he thought it was too much, but I insisted. I sent a cashier's check for $2,000 as an earnest money deposit and asked for 90 days to close. They sent it back with a note that they would consider a serious offer when they got one. Mr. Smart was obviously relieved that they didn't make a counter offer, but he almost fainted when I told him to raise the offer to $50,000.

They sent that offer back with a letter saying they would not take a penny less than the assessed valuation of $55,000. They said I could reduce the deposit to $1,000 and have three months to produce the rest of the cash, but there would be no contingencies except for good title. Tommy Dickson wanted to share the deal with me, but his wife vetoed it. She did not want a partner and neither did I.

Before making another offer, I consulted various moonlighters: a plumber, a floor refinisher, a roofer, a linoleum man, and a painter. I got a free termite inspection and found there had been an infestation in the past, but there was no serious damage and there were no termites now. I got written estimates from all these moonlighters and arrived at an approximate cost to put the property in condition to rent. I had been warned not to spend too much, because I would not get enough additional rent to make a difference. And I wanted to avoid unnecessary improvements known as "gold door knobs" in the appraising trade. This means they cost extra money but add very little to the market value.

I went to my banker at the First and Merchants bank where we kept our personal account. I was lucky that he had some vision and imagination. He said that if I could get a commitment for the permanent financing he could make me a temporary loan to buy it. Then when the improvements were made, I could place the permanent loan and pay him off. He referred me to the Home Beneficial Life Insurance Company, a small, privately-owned company with headquarters in Richmond.

We still had the house in Fairfax County, Virginia, and I was sure we could sell it within a couple of months. I presented to Home Beneficial the projections for cost of improvements, rental income, and operating expenses. They said they felt sure they would lend me $45,000 once I made the improvements and rented the apartments. They could not process a loan application, however, until I had a contract to buy it.

Next I went to Cameron Brown, a second-mortgage specialist in Richmond. The local manager had a problem with his teeth or his gums, and he had his jaws temporarily wired together. He looked the building over and listened to my plans. He said he thought I was going to have a gold mine there. His words were like music to me, even though he had to speak them with his teeth clenched. He agreed to lend the other $10,000 on a second mortgage once I made all the improvements and rented the apartments.

The money from the sale of the Fairfax County house was to be used for improvements. First and Merchants Bank and Cameron Brown would lend me enough to cover the purchase price and also give me 90 days to make the improvements for the permanent financing. Jeff Fell, one of my friends at the office, was keenly interested in what I was doing. He kept asking questions:

"What happens if you can't get your first mortgage?"

"I lose my deposit."

"What happens if you can't get your second mortgage?"

"I lose my deposit."

"Why didn't you make the contract contingent on getting these mortgages?"

"I tried, but the owners would not agree to it."

"How can you risk your deposit with no more protection than you have?"

I told him I had studied this from every angle, and I believed there was a 90 percent chance everything would work out fine. I asked him if he would be willing to bet a thousand dollars that he could pick a white marble out of a box blindfolded, if he knew there were nine white marbles in the box and only one black one. He thought for a long time. "I guess I would bet," he finally said, "but I would be scared to death." I told him I was scared too, but there was no way to be successful without taking some risks.

After doing all this, I went back to my lawyer and told him to prepare the contract for the amount of the assessed valuation with $1,000 earnest money deposit for settlement in 90 days and no contingencies except for marketable title. He was visibly shaken when I told him. He wrote it under protest, all the time muttering under his breath as if it were his own money at risk. After the contract was signed by all parties, Tommy Dickson offered me $1,500 cash if I would assign the contract to him.

"Boy, you are lucky," Mr. Smart said. "You made money on it." I told him I had refused the offer, and he just shook his head and walked off. I guess he was thinking, "That's when two fools met." I learned later that some other people in Richmond had been trying to buy the building at about the same time. If I had not gone ahead and paid the price, I could easily have lost the deal.

We set a below-market price on the house in Fairfax County and easily sold it within two weeks. It was much more important to have a quick sale than to milk another 10 percent out of the price. We then went to settlement on the building. The bank loaned most of the money on a 90-day note secured by a first mortgage, and Cameron-Brown loaned the rest of the purchase price. I gave them a 90-day note secured by a blanket second mortgage on both the building and our home, with the home to be released from the mortgage after the improvements were made.

The building had only six parking spaces. That was all the zoning required when it was built, but the laws had since changed. The current use was allowed under a grandfather clause; but if the building had been destroyed, it could not have been rebuilt without major changes. Since a man had been living in one of the front rooms for about 15 years, using it as an efficiency unit, I went to the city zoning authorities and asked for a new use permit to allow me to rent the six front bedrooms as efficiency apartments. After I documented the facts, they issued me a use permit for 12 three-room apartments and six one-room apartments. The lack of parking spaces was not a serious problem, because the bus stop was one block away and most of the tenants did not have cars.

After we had the title, we had 90 more days to improve and convert the apartments in order to place the permanent financing. For that, we used the money from the sale of the house. I could buy a good used bedroom set with box springs and mattress for a $150, a used apartment-sized refrigerator for $40, and a sofa, coffee table, easy chair, and two end tables for not much over $100. I had to buy refrigerators for all the efficiencies, but the other apartments already had refrigerators and gas stoves. I learned I could buy a used but serviceable gas stove for about $25; so if a thermostat went bad on one, I just replaced the stove instead of calling a repair service.

No cooking was allowed in the six efficiencies. But I put a small used refrigerator in each one, along with a sofa, coffee table, and a couple of chairs. The sofa was a twin bed with a bolster next to the wall. With the bolster on, it was a sofa. With the bolster off, it was a bed. All six efficiencies had private baths and entrances from the front porch. They also had a door to the other bedroom, but we nailed those doors shut. That converted the building from 12 units to 18 units. Some of the tenants in the efficiencies later got hotplates, but I never had official notice of that and I chose to look the other way.

I ran ads in the paper and bought used stuff from homes, and I went to estate sales and garage sales until I got all that I needed. I had plenty of annual leave available, so I took two weeks off from my job to do all this. I used U-Haul trailers, and sometimes a rented truck, to move the stuff to the apartments. I hired a couple of out-of-work laborers to help me.

I rented all of them furnished and by the week. That produced twice as much income as when I bought it, even if it had been full then. I owned that building eight years and got the annual income up another 50 percent by the time I sold it. I had to pay all the utility bills, but that still left a substantial profit.

The money from the Fairfax house sale paid for enough improvements to place the permanent financing. The first mortgage was at 9 percent for 15 years. That was high interest and short term, but I was happy to get it. I paid 10 percent interest on the second mortgage, and had much of it paid off before we sold. The bank used Home Beneficial's mortgage forms to make the temporary loan, and that made it easier to switch over when Home Beneficial took over the permanent financing. Cameron-Brown released the second mortgage on our home as soon as the improvements were made and the permanent financing was in place.

We refinished all the floors, repaired the roof, put inlaid linoleum in all the kitchens and baths, and painted the apartment walls. We painted everything with latex paint in oyster white. It took four coats of white to completely hide the black paint in that one apartment. Luckily, the plaster walls were in good condition throughout the building and all the electric wiring was fairly new.

We replaced the hang-on sinks with self-contained metal units by Youngstown Kitchens. They each had a sink, drainboards on either side, storage space underneath, and two cabinets above—all in one unit. In some settings they would have looked cheap and tinny; but they were inexpensive and much nicer than what was there before. I put shower rings, mounted on poles, over the bathtubs, installed shower curtains, and ran flexible metal hoses from the faucets to the shower heads.

I eventually got a personal signature loan from the bank to finish all we wanted to do and to buy the rest of the used furniture. I had an adequate income to live on from my job in the Immigration Service, so we had plenty of rental income to make improvements and to repay the loans. I did all the collecting and renting for about a year, and then made a deal with one of the tenants to do that in return for free rent.

Several of the tenants let their empty bottles collect on their back porches, so I asked if they would like me to remove them. Most of them agreed. From then on, I took my kids there once a week and let them gather up all the bottles that were outside the building on the back porches. We took them to a store where the kids turned them in for extra spending money. Soft drinks came in glass bottles in those days and they charged a two-cent deposit on each bottle if you took it out of the store.

For the last four years of ownership, I lived in another city. I kept in touch with things through the resident manager, but I had a problem with him. His name was Owens, and I wondered about him from the first, because he never talked about where he came from and he always had an unlisted phone number. He was living with a woman who passed as his wife, but I sometimes wondered about that too.

Because of my concern, I bought a big receipt book that provided three copies of each receipt. They were about five inches long and three inches wide, and they were color coded according to where each copy went. I instructed him to give one copy to the tenant, keep one copy for his records, and send the other copy to me along with the bank deposit slips.

About a year after I had moved to Washington, I noticed we were having an unusual number of vacancies. I called Tommy Dickson to see if he was having the same problem, and he was surprised by my question. He said he had no vacancy problems whatever. I then analyzed the records for the past several months, and found one apartment that showed a vacancy three times, and each vacancy lasted exactly two weeks. Other apartments had similar records.

I made a surprise visit to the building one evening and knocked on the door of that apartment. The tenant told me he had lived there for more than a year, and he had never missed a rent payment during that time. He showed me rent receipts for several months, and each one was from a little dime-store receipt book.

My manager had been keeping a separate set of books for me, and giving receipts to the tenants from a different receipt book. He reported to me only what he did not keep for himself. When he kept the money from one of the apartments, he showed it as vacant in my records and wrote one of his own little receipts for the occupant. I later figured he embezzled several hundred dollars, and possibly a lot more.

I thought about having him arrested but finally decided against it. His wife didn't always seem to be all there, and I was uneasy about going to court against them. Also, I had a good job in the headquarters of the immigration service in Washington. My bosses knew about the apartment building, and there was nothing illegal or unethical about it. But any legal action would have brought publicity that might have been embarrassing to the government. Any judgment I might get against him would be worthless, so I decided to eat my losses and chalk it up to experience. "If you have to eat a live frog, eat it quick"

I went to see him at his apartment one morning and told him I wanted the receipt books and all the rent money he had collected and I wanted him out by midnight that night. I told him I had conclusive evidence he had been stealing from me. And if he didn't move out by that night, I would prosecute him for grand theft. I also warned him not to take any more rent payments from the tenants. I guess he could not resist one more caper, and he collected and kept the rent from three more tenants before he left. He left no forwarding address and had his new telephone unlisted, so I suppose he thought I could not find him.

But he had lived in one of the two-bedroom, two-bath apartments on the ground floor, and I had allowed him to put a washing machine in the front bathroom on the condition that he pay his own electric deposit and pay the monthly bills himself. After he moved, he applied for a refund of his deposit. That made it easy for me to find him, and the electric company even had his phone number. When I called him at his unlisted phone number and told him I knew where he lived, he sent me the rest of my money at once.

After that I used a couple named Chevrette as managers, and I never had a minute's trouble with them. They rarely reported a vacancy, and even then it was usually filled within a couple of days. He worked full-time and she did not, so she was there during the day to show apartments to prospective tenants. They kept the job until I sold the building, and I recommended them highly to the buyers.

I bought that building in 1966 and sold it in 1974. I used the money from the sale of the house in Fairfax County and borrowed the rest to buy it. The income from it paid back my loans and put our oldest son through college, and I sold it for two-and-a-half times what I paid for it. The cashier's check from the sale was enough for the down payment on the 30 units I later bought in Florida.

Yet, I had to fight with my lawyer to make him submit the contracts to buy it, and I paid $15,000 more for it than the highest price my professional appraiser said I should pay. But John Elam told me I stole it, and Tommy Dickson, who already owned several buildings, offered me $1,500 for my contract. "Expert" advice can sometimes be wrong.

♠ ♠ ♠ ♠

A man who had been successful in the stock market once said you cannot expect to buy at the bottom of the market and to sell at the top. He said many times he felt he had paid too much for stocks and sold them too soon. The same applies to real estate. If you buy only when you can get a price below the market you won't buy much real estate. And if you buy only property that is in apple-pie condition, you will have a difficult time increasing its market value. You have to pay prime prices to buy prime properties, and then you have to wait for inflation to raise the market value.

A man named Nickerson had the right idea in the book he wrote about 40 years ago. He said the best bargains are sound, well-located buildings that are priced lower because they need cosmetic improvements. Then, every dollar spent on improvements can add two or three dollars to the market value. On the other hand, you could spend many thousands of dollars on hidden structural repairs without making the property look any better. It is best to avoid buildings like that.

♠ ♠ ♠ ♠

Owning an apartment building is not an easy way to get rich. One reason I am writing this is to show how much work, worry, and aggravation can be involved. If big profits could be realized by passive investments in real estate, the banks and insurance companies would own most of it. There was a saying in Florida that the footprints of the owner are the best fertilizer an orange grove could have. If he is on the scene an owner can see the problems and take measures to correct them. The same logic applies to apartment buildings.

If there are only 30 or 40 units in an apartment building, a professional management company will take a substantial share of the profits. They will want a resident manager to show the apartments and collect the rents. They will give the manager free rent and a salary in addition. Management companies charge a percentage of total rents for overseeing the operation, and they often also charge a percentage of anything they spend on repairs and maintenance. They may hide the charges within the bills, but they will be there. Each time a faucet starts to drip, it will cost an hour's pay for a plumber to come and replace a 10-cent washer.

A large complex needs an office staffed with professional managers. It may also need a maintenance staff to take care of day-to-day problems. Even though the management costs will be significant, the percentage of these costs in relation to total income will be lower than with a small complex. Most major investors in apartments will not consider anything with fewer than 100 units, and more is better.

♠ ♠ ♠ ♠

After we had been in Washington a few months, I heard of a job opportunity in Richmond at a higher grade than I had when I was there before. I was told I would get the job and my wife did not like living in Washington, so we went back to Richmond to look at houses. We found a house on Monmouth Court with four bedrooms, two baths, and a one-car garage, all on one level and on a tree-covered lot. It was for sale by the owners, and we negotiated with them in their living room. We were about $1,000 apart, and I did not want to go any higher because my wife hated the chartreuse wall-to-wall carpet in the living room and I knew we would have to replace it. They would not accept my offer because they said they had just spent over $1,000 on the new carpet. I could not tell them we didn't like it and would have to rip it out, because that would have been criticizing their taste. So I offered to let them keep it if they would accept our offer, and they agreed. They may have had no use for that carpet in the future, but at least they saved face. I would have paid them to take it out if it had been necessary.

Because of some changed circumstances, I did not get the job in Richmond. So I was still working in Washington while living 100 miles away. At first, I rented a small apartment and came home on weekends and on Wednesday nights, to break up the week. In the meantime, Ken Temple, who had worked in Richmond for years, got promoted to Washington. We decided to carpool together and we commuted daily to Washington for several months, over 100 miles each way. Finally, we bought another house that was near Washington and sold the one in Richmond. We made some money on the sale, but not much.

A Tour Of Duty In Arizona

LESSON 18: There are few things you can do to a house that will increase the value by more than the cost of the improvement. Most of them are cosmetic, and, for example, a swimming pool is a luxury that most buyers will not pay for.

In June 1972, I volunteered for a transfer to Phoenix, Arizona. I drove out, stayed a month, and then flew back and moved my family after the house sold. I stayed in Flagstaff the last night of the trip to Phoenix, and when I left at 8:00 a.m., the next morning the temperature was 32 degrees. The elevation at Flagstaff is 7,000 feet, and at Phoenix 1,000 feet. In that two-hour ride over a distance of 100 miles, the temperature rose from 32 degrees to more than 100 degrees.

Phoenix sits in a natural bowl with mountains all around. At one time it was known for its clean air, but eventually smog became a problem. A dam across the Salt River formed a lake that collected the runoff from the rains and snows in the surrounding mountains. The water from that lake irrigated the farmlands in the area, as well as lawns and golf courses in Phoenix. They obtained irrigation water also from Lake Mead, the reservoir behind Hoover Dam on the Colorado River. The combination of the irrigation water and the hot sun put humidity into the air, and that moisture combined with dust and smoke particles to create smog.

We drove out of the city one day and went to a steak house up in the mountains. After we climbed a few hundred feet we were in clear air again, But when we looked back at the city, the smog at the lower levels made it look like a bowl half full of some smoky-looking liquid. When the wind blows, it takes the smog out of the bowl; but when there is no wind, the smog can stay for days.

I played golf one weekend with three other men from the Immigration office. We started at eight o'clock in the morning, and they opened big golf umbrellas and installed them on the golf carts. I wondered what they were thinking of, because there had not been any rain for almost three months. I soon learned the umbrellas were for protection against the hot sun. The name parasol comes from para sol, meaning "for sun" in Spanish.

♠ ♠ ♠ ♠

Soon after I arrived, I ran an ad in the newspaper saying I was transferring there and wanted to buy a house. I got a few calls and eventually bought a house from a couple who hadn't decided to sell but had been thinking about it. I got good financing from a local bank and even got them to include a swimming pool to be installed, complete with a gas-fired heater and with an automatic cleaning system. I made a contract with a local pool company and the bank appraised the house as if the pool were already in the ground. I financed the whole thing with 10 percent down, and the bank held back enough money in an escrow account to pay for the pool when it was completed.

The pool was a mistake in our case. Jody was away at college, and David and Melissa were in the pool every day for two or three weeks and then lost interest. When my brother Bruce and his family came to visit from Idaho for two weeks, their three kids and our kids were in the pool constantly. After they went home, the pool was not used again. I turned on the pool heater in March and kept the water warm for a month, but the pool was not used during that time. Even in south Florida where many houses have pools, few of them get much use. To some, a pool is worth the money although most kids prefer to go to the beach, or to the homes of friends for swimming parties.

When we moved from Phoenix to Miami a year later, we lost a few hundred dollars on the sale of that house, solely because of the $6,000 I had spent on the pool. Two things saved us from losing more. One was buying from an owner at a good price. The other was having the immigration service pay all our selling expenses as a part of my transfer costs.

Following the installment sale of the 30 units when I was 63, the investment income from real estate allowed me to seriously pursue my hobby of competitive pistol shooting. Each of these six trophies represents a Senior National Championship won at the National Matches held by the National Rifle Association each year at Camp Perry, Ohio. The minimum age to compete as a Senior is 60, and my first championship came at age 64 and the last at 70. (photo by Joseph C. White)

Arizona Rental Property

LESSON 19: The "economy of scale" does not always work out. Bigger is not always better in real estate management.

LESSON 20: Be wary of investing heavily in an area where the economy depends primarily on one industry. If that industry falls on hard times, the hard times may extend to you.

When we went to Phoenix I was nearing retirement eligibility, so we thought about staying there. There were many apartment buildings in the Phoenix area and a reasonable amount of buying and selling. I considered retiring and getting a real estate-license in Arizona, thinking I would specialize in apartment buildings. I would then replace the Richmond building with one in Phoenix, to get away from the long-distance management problems.

Several things were different in Arizona. The climate was so dry there was no concern about dampness from the ground, except for an occasional flood. They built many of the apartment buildings on concrete slabs placed on the ground. They put footings around the perimeter and under the bearing walls, and there was no crawl space. On the ground floor they often put padding and carpets directly on the concrete slabs.

Many of the apartment buildings had central systems that were run by electricity, combining the functions of heating and air conditioning. The winters were not severe, and heating was not a major problem. Air conditioning costs were high, however, because of the intense summer heat and because this was a period of rising electric rates. The building owners usually paid all the utility bills since it was not easy to calculate the cost for each tenant. Most of them simply increased the rental rates to cover the utilities.

Much of the countryside around Phoenix is hilly, and roadside signs warn motorists to be alert for flash floods. There are few bridges across the small streams because they are usually dry. A careless motorist may come to the bottom of a hill and suddenly find himself in water up to his chin. These dry stream beds often carry water from rainstorms far away in the mountains. We had a flood in Phoenix once when it had not rained at all near the city. The rainwater from the surrounding mountains followed the irrigation canals into the city. It overflowed all the canals and ditches and caused heavy damage.

♠ ♠ ♠ ♠

I looked at a 26-unit apartment building that floodwaters had damaged. Flood insurance had paid for all the repairs. I tried to buy it, using my equity in the Richmond building as the down payment, but it didn't work out. The seller was suspicious of trades, especially when the other property was located so far away. I did not have a ready buyer for the Richmond property at the time, and that may have been an even bigger problem.

I watched the classified ads for a few days and identified a broker who was specializing in apartment buildings. I went to see him and told him I might retire in Phoenix and would like to affiliate with his company. He invited me to join a discussion group on investing that was held in his offices at night. That's how I met Bill Riley. He was being paid by the broker to lead the discussion group and to talk about his experiences with apartment buildings. He had been reduced to this after being a multimillionaire apartment owner in Seattle. He was about 40 years old, intelligent, and very articulate.

Mr. Riley had been a bricklayer, then a masonry contractor, and later a general contractor. He had gone to Seattle when the Boeing

Aircraft Company was expanding because of massive government contracts. He said he commissioned a demographic study that revealed a need for a 200-300 unit apartment complex in a certain area. He arranged his permanent financing and his temporary construction loan, and built 218 units. His construction costs, his projected operating expenses, and his debt-service payments made it a successful venture based on his projected rents if he had 90 percent occupancy. By the time it was finished and the permanent financing was in place, he had them all rented for even higher rents and had a long waiting list.

But he did not know that others were doing the same demographic study at the same time. Within a year, there were a thousand other units under construction within two miles of his apartments. At one time he had refused an offer of $2 million for his position in the apartment complex. "Don't be silly," he had replied. "It's worth a lot more than that."

A couple of years later Boeing lost most of their government contracts for airplanes and laid-off a huge number of their employees. That caused the bottom to drop out of the economy there. Many of Riley's tenants lost their jobs and could not pay their rent. He said on the main road leading out of Seattle there was a big sign: "THE LAST ONE OUT OF TOWN PLEASE TURN OUT THE LIGHTS!" He could not rent his apartments, could not make his mortgage payments, and could not sell the property. He had to give his apartments to the mortgage company, and he came back to Phoenix broke.

While things were still going well, Riley had set his father up as a management company with a contract to manage his 218 units. It went well, and Riley was pleased with the results. His father then expanded and took over another complex to manage, but he had to hire an assistant. After a while he was managing a thousand units and was losing money, because business was bad and the costs of doing business increased faster than the additional income. He eventually gave up the management business

I always wanted to be a builder and developer, but I never had the talent for either one. One man I envy has had great success with both, my wife's brother Harvey Coleman, pictured above with his wife Charmie. He learned apartment development through the family operation in Washington, D.C. After successful association with several national development firms, Harvey became involved in the acquisition and production of income-producing real estate nationwide, and was the operational head in design and development of a number of residential condominium units in Florida. A recognized executive in solving corporate real estate problems, he led the goal-achieving work of a prominent real estate investment trust. When headquartered in Atlanta, he was General Partner in a series of profitable syndications that acquired, developed, and operated office complexes, speciality projects, hotels, land packages, and apartment projects across the Southeastern states. Harvey is now retired and lives in Maryland. (photo courtesy of Joseph C. White)

Thirty Units In Florida

LESSON 21: "A confused mind says no" is more than just a saying. Make your deal as simple as possible with a minimum of complications.

I transferred from Phoenix to Miami in 1973 and bought a house in Hollywood, 20 miles north of Miami. We planned to continue to live in Hollywood after retirement, so I decided to sell the building in Richmond and buy one in Florida. A Realtor® in Richmond named Charles A. Rose had made inquiries about buying it, and we had preliminary talks that sounded promising.

After several weeks of looking and comparing, I saw 30 units in Broward County for sale by the builders. This property consisted of two buildings. Each building had two levels, with half of the apartments upstairs and the other half downstairs. A swimming pool with a fence around it sat between the two buildings. The back boundary of the property was a canal 25 feet wide. A concrete seawall on each side guided the canal to the Middle River, which went to the Atlantic Ocean. A bridge crossed the canal about two blocks downstream. It could not be raised to let boats pass, so traffic was usually limited to boats no longer than 16 feet.

One of the buildings had 12 units and was built in 1970. It had 6 one-bedroom, one-bath apartments; 5 two-bedroom, bath-and-a-half apartments; and 1 three-bedroom, two-bath apartment. A laundry room on the ground floor had two washers and two dryers, all coin operated. The space on the second floor over the laundry room was the third bedroom of the one apartment. There was a separate meter room on the end of the building behind the laundry room. This meter room housed 13 electric meters, one for the building and one each for the 12 apartments.

The second building had 18 units and was built one year later, in 1971. Four of the apartments, two up and two down, were smaller than the others and formed an L at one end of the building. Another L completed the other end of the building. On the ground floor was a laundry room like the one in the first building, except there were three washers. Next to the laundry room, a meter room housed 19 electric meters, one for the building and one each for the 18 units. A small room on the second floor over the laundry room provided storage space. An electric water heater in each laundry room furnished hot water for the washing machines.

One building was three years old and the other was four. The existing mortgage was only a year old, and I assumed the builders had combined the mortgages on the two buildings after they were fully rented and well established. They probably had mortgaged-out (re-financed for enough to repay them for their total investment in both buildings.)

The property was in Wilton Manors, a suburb of Fort Lauderdale, Florida. It was in a neighborhood of small, unpretentious, single-family homes, and the apartments were only a block from the city hall and the police station. Next door was an 18-unit apartment building, and a block away was a 24-unit building with a pool. Two blocks away was a high-rise apartment building with perhaps 100 units. It was eight stories high and had been built as a condominium for the members of a religious organization. That did not work out financially, so they converted it to a rental complex.

One of the owners of the 30 units had a real-estate license, but he was taking no commission. I had no agent helping me, so I expected to get at least a 3 percent reduction from the asking price, and maybe 6 percent. They had advertised it for $18,000 a unit, but after some discussion they agreed to take $17,000, since there was no commission to pay. I asked them to consider a like-property exchange under Section 1031 of the Federal Tax Code, if I could provide a cash buyer ready to pay them at closing for the Richmond property. I explained that it would not cost them anything and it would be a tax break for me. I could then defer the capital gains tax on the profit from the Richmond sale until such time as I sold this building. They were uneasy about that, especially since the other property was in another state. I soon concluded they would sell for less if we kept the transaction as simple as possible.

♠ ♠ ♠ ♠

Meanwhile, the Realtor® in Richmond and his partner submitted a firm offer that met my price and terms, so I was able to talk serious business. I wrote an offer on a blank contract form (I got it from a title insurance company) that was approved by the bar association of Broward County. We had sold a house, so we had some cash on hand. I drew a cashier's check for $5,000, made out to myself, and attached it to my offer. I wrote the contract for 10 percent less than their asking price, using the proceeds from the Richmond sale as the down payment. I offered to assume the first mortgage and give the sellers a second mortgage for the balance at 10 percent interest, with interest-only payments each month and payment in full in 10 years.

The seller was a corporation consisting of three brothers, their mother, and their wives. The brothers and I discussed the deal for at least an hour. For a long time they were insisting on $17,000 a unit. I said it might be worth that much, but I could not afford to pay the price. I came up to a little over $16,000 a unit and held my ground there. If we argued about what the property was worth, they might have an advantage over me. But if we argued about what I could afford, I had a stronger position. "If we are going to take this offer," one of them finally said, "we ought to at least get the second mortgage paid off in five years instead of 10." I then agreed to pay interest only for the first five years and to pay off the mortgage in equal payments over the following five years.

The contract was contingent on my getting the money from the sale in Richmond. They agreed to this because there was already a firm contract on that property. We signed the contract and I endorsed the cashier's check to them as earnest money. I think the cashier's check helped make the deal because they did not want me to leave and take it with me. If it had been a personal check for a smaller amount, they would have wondered if I was serious and might not have reduced their price.

We closed the Richmond sale by mail. We got a cashier's check from Richmond one morning and then went to Fort Lauderdale and closed on the 30 units that afternoon. We made these arrangements in advance, because we didn't want that money lying around. With my permission, they dissolved their corporation and the individual people signed the deed. That gave them a tax benefit and it didn't matter to me.

♣ ♣ ♣ ♣

I could not use the rollover rule to defer capital gains taxes on the Richmond sale, because that applied only to principal residences. Some would say I should have insisted on working out a tax-deferred exchange to delay the tax consequences, but things aren't always so easy to arrange, especially when one property is located in another state.

[A court decision in the Starker case and the subsequent IRS interpretations now provide a method that makes tax-deferred exchanges easier. The proceeds of the sale of an investment property can go directly into an escrow fund and be held there by a third party until it is used to pay for the replacement investment property. The seller has 45 days to identify the replacement property and 180 days to complete the transaction. Discuss this with an attorney or an escrow company familiar with the process before you sign a contract. I don't recall when this case was decided, but it was either too late for me to use it at the time or else I had not heard about it yet.]

The same logic applies when buying a house with the purchase offer contingent on the sale of your old house. That is a safe way to buy, although you cannot get the best deal in most cases. You can always drive a harder bargain when the seller knows if he signs that contract the house is almost certainly sold. That is especially true when the seller is under pressure to sell and when time is important. But if you sell first and have a deadline to move, you had better have a temporary residence available or you may have to pay too much for another place because of the pressure to find a place to go.

Tax-deferred exchanges are available under Section 1031 only to like-kind properties. But it can be different kinds of investment property such as vacant land for apartment buildings, or orange groves for warehouses, or rental houses, for example. But it does not work for trading a personal residence or a mortgage.

Since the two buildings were on a wide canal with access to Middle River, I named the buildings Riverview East and Riverview West and put prominent signs on them. I could not very well name them simply Riverview Apartments, because there was another building a few blocks away with that name.

This is the 30 units in Florida bought in 1974 using a down payment from sale of the Richmond, Virginia property and a purchase money second mortgage. The upper photo is the 12 units on NE 20th Street in Wilton Manor in Ft. Lauderdale, Florida, and the lower photo is of the 18 units. They provided a substantial cash flow for eight plus years until I refinanced the second mortgage in 1981 and took out $95,000 net. The two buildings were sold in late 1983 for $1 million, with net down payment and mortgage taken back totaling well over half of the sale price. (photos by Joseph C. White)

Winning One From The IRS

*LESSON 22: Stand up for your rights! IRS does not always win.
I think their agents use any rule that comes close to applying if it
is against the interest of the taxpayer. They feel safe about being
strict, but don't dare be too lenient. They prefer to reject all
arguments and make the taxpayer prove them wrong. Many
taxpayers give up rather than fight.*

We bought the Broward County 30 units in the spring of 1974, and
I retired from the Immigration Service in October of that year.
There would be no income taxes on my retirement annuity until
after I got back all my contributions to the retirement fund. I knew
my annuity would be tax-free at least for the balance of 1974 and
all of 1975, but I had a significant tax liability for 1974. I had the
profit on the Richmond sale, my salary until my retirement, and the
cash payment for 67 days of unused annual leave. I expected to
pay no income tax whatever for 1975 because my annuity would
be tax-free for that year and I would get depreciation on the
apartment building to offset any profit.

IRS allows the owner of investment building to take a tax loss each
year for the wearing out of the building. This is called depreciation
and it is not an actual cash loss. IRS says land does not depreciate,
so the value of the land must be deducted before calculating the
depreciation. The tax assessor makes one valuation for the land
and another valuation for the buildings. Using his ratio as a guide, I
estimated I paid 18 percent of the cost for the land and 82 percent
for the buildings.

At that time, IRS allowed the owner to estimate the remaining economic life of the building, so long as IRS considered it reasonable. (I had estimated 15 years on the Richmond building, and IRS allowed it because it was 50 years old at the time and because the longest mortgage I could get was 15 years.) I estimated 25 years on the 30 units and set up the depreciation schedule based on that, allowing me to show for tax purposes a paper loss each year of 1/25 (4 percent) of the cost of the buildings. Accordingly, it was possible to enjoy a cash flow of many thousands of dollars a year and still show a loss for tax purposes. There were many complicated ways you could depreciate a building at the time. Each had certain advantages and disadvantages, and most are no longer in effect. I chose straight-line depreciation because it was simplest and gave a better tax break at the end. Depreciation deductions are not permanent gifts from IRS, because they are part of your capital gain when you sell.

I knew I would have a significant tax liability for 1974 but would have none for 1975, so I looked for some way to transfer deductions from 1975 and move them back into 1974. Accordingly, in December 1974 I made the monthly mortgage payment that was due January 2, 1975, and claimed the interest deduction in 1974. The IRS did not like that.

Regardless of when the payment was made, the bank that held the first mortgage always charged a month's interest on the day the payment was due and added that amount to the principal balance of the mortgage. If they received the payment exactly on the second day of the month, they applied the interest portion to interest and the principal portion to principal. If they received it at any other time, they applied the total payment to reduce the principal balance. In either case, they added the interest charge to the principal on the second day of the month, the exact date the payment was due.

♠ ♠ ♠ ♠

Broward Federal, the first mortgage holder, was reporting to IRS on the accrual basis, and that was legitimate. They reported the interest as if it had been received on the date it came due, regardless of when it was paid. That system was less complicated for the bank, and IRS allowed it. But I reported on the cash basis, as most individual taxpayers do. I reported interest expense as of the date I paid it, regardless of when it was due. I could not claim a deduction for interest in any year unless I paid it during that year. My monthly payment included principal, interest, and an escrow payment for taxes and insurance.

When I sent my January payment in December, I itemized on the check the amount of principal and the amount of interest. Broward Federal cashed my check and got the money out of my checking account long before the end of the year. They followed their usual practice and applied the interest portion to the reduction of principal. Then on January 2, 1975, they charged the interest to me and added that amount back to the principal.

Therefore, when they sent my statement of interest paid during 1974, the interest for the early January 1975 payment was not included. Nevertheless, I showed that canceled check to my CPA and told him to add that interest to the amount the bank said I had paid. He said I was right and it should be counted, but he warned that I should be prepared for IRS to challenge it.

Subsequently, IRS called me for an audit of my apartment building accounts for 1974. That was not surprising, since it was my first year of ownership. I didn't worry because I had all the income and expenses well documented, and I had paid the capital-gains taxes on the Richmond sale. I showed the auditor the canceled check for the January payment and told him I had paid it in December and claimed that interest payment in 1974. The check was stamped on the back showing that Broward Federal got their money in December 1974. The auditor said I could not claim the deduction for 1974 because the tax court had ruled that a taxpayer cannot claim an interest deduction unless the bank considers it interest. I asked him for a copy of that ruling but he did not have it.

That was the only thing he questioned. He said I owed more than $900 in additional taxes for 1974 because of the disallowed interest deduction for that January payment. He said his hands were tied because he had to follow the rule that there is no tax deduction for interest if the bank does not consider it interest. I then appealed the case to the next higher level of IRS.

♠ ♠ ♠ ♠

I had two or three meetings with them, all with the same result. Eventually they gave me a copy of the court ruling they relied on, and it was totally off the point. That case concerned a man who had obtained a loan at a bank and had been required to take out a life insurance policy in favor of the bank as added security for the loan. The borrower was required to make an additional insurance payment in December to bring the policy current, but when he made the December <u>mortgage</u> payment, he wrote "for interest only" on the check. The bank did not credit that payment to interest, but used it instead to pay the insurance premium that was due, in accordance with his contract with the bank. The tax court ruling disallowed the deduction because the bank used the money for the insurance premium and did not consider it interest.

IRS insisted I owed the extra money plus accrued interest. I talked to a lawyer, but he wanted a thousand dollars for a retainer, and that was more than what IRS said I owed. Obviously that was not the answer.

I wrote letters to IRS and argued my case. I pointed out that the cited case was different from mine. I had learned from my years in the immigration service that a case has to be "on all fours" with another case to be controlling, and this one was not. In this sense, on all fours means alike in every respect. In the case they cited, the payment never became interest. The bank used it first and always as the required payment for the insurance premium, even though that was not what the taxpayer intended. In my case the payment did become interest.

The bank had the money since mid-December, but they counted it as a principal payment when they got it. Then on January 2, they took it out of their principal account and put it into their interest account. It was simply a matter of <u>when</u> the bank considered it interest. That fit their accounting system because the bank used the accrual method. Since I used the cash method of reporting, the law required me to report the interest when I actually paid it. That obviously was in December 1974. At that time it was legal to deduct interest paid in advance, although I think that law was changed the following year.

IRS finally wrote me a letter demanding payment in full but did say I had the option of taking the case to the tax court. The letter said my reply must be received by IRS, or postmarked, within a certain number of days in order to get a hearing in tax court. They sent the notice by certified mail. The tax court was located in Tampa, Florida and I was living in Washington, D.C. at the time.

I thought about it a long time and finally sent my claim by certified mail on the last day allowed. IRS wrote back and said I had missed my chance to go to tax court because my letter had been received after the deadline and it was not postmarked before the deadline. When I sent my certified letter, the post office had given me a dated receipt but had not stamped a postmark. IRS was trying to use that technicality against me.

I replied that they sent their notice to me by certified mail and there was no postmark. Furthermore, I received it <u>after</u> the response period started running. Since they relied on a certified mail receipt to start the time running when they sent me their notice, I could certainly rely on a certified mail receipt for the time of my response. I sent them a copy of my mailing receipt to prove I had mailed it in time. I said if it became necessary, I would take the case to federal court on the grounds that IRS was denying my constitutional right to due process.

I argued that a first-year law student could tell them their position was untenable. I asked which of their lawyers wanted to stand before a federal judge and try to explain it. They finally relented and scheduled me for a hearing in the tax court in Tampa. I was bluffing, of course, because I didn't know that much about the law. But their position violated all the rules of fairness and common sense and I did not see how they could get away with it.

♠ ♠ ♠ ♠

There was another minor problem. The following year, 1975, I had no income for tax purposes. My annuity was not yet taxable, and the building showed a loss after taking the depreciation allowance. When my CPA did the tax return he used the statement from the bank for the interest deduction, and we both forgot that it included the interest on that one payment which I was claiming in the prior year. I still would owe no tax, but IRS made an issue of it.

A week before I was to leave for the hearing, I got a call from IRS. The caller asked if I planned to go to the hearing and I said yes. He asked if I had a lawyer and I said no, that I thought the IRS position was so unreasonable that I could argue the case myself and win easily. He then said IRS would drop the assessment for the extra tax if I would file an amended return for 1975 and remove the deduction for that one-month's interest I had previously claimed in 1974. I said I would be glad to do that; but it would make no difference, because there would still be no tax to pay. He said IRS still wanted that amended return, just to keep the record straight. My CPA charged me $35 to file the amended return; there still was no tax to pay. The IRS wrote me a letter stating I had no further tax liability for 1974. IRS didn't make a dime on that audit, and so far I have never been audited since.

Negotiating A Big Contract

LESSON 23: If you get an offer or a counteroffer, and you are getting a good deal, it does not pay to try to nickel-and-dime the other party. You may lose the contract by doing so, as these buyers learned the hard way. The same applies whether buying or selling. If the offer is fair and you can live with it, accept it as it is. Buyer's remorse or seller's remorse can strike quickly. But if you wouldn't mind losing the deal, you can afford to gamble.

After I had the Broward County 30-unit property about a year, a broker named Joe Poffenberg called me and said he had someone who wanted to buy it. He had been active in converting apartments to condominiums, and I had a few discussions with him when I first started looking at buildings in Florida. He had told me I got a good buy after I bought this one. I set a price that would net me a nice profit and allowed him to show it, with the stipulation that there would be no commission paid unless a sale was actually closed.

The buyers made an offer considerably lower than what I had asked, and they wanted to assume the first and second mortgages and give me a third mortgage. I made a counteroffer near my original price. The buyers had a lawyer who was known as a tough negotiator, but they signed my counteroffer with only two new conditions. One was that I make a small repair that I had told the broker I would make anyway and the other that the buyers take title and give me a third mortgage in the name of a general partnership instead of as individuals. That didn't concern me, because they both would still have been individually liable.

But by then I was suffering from seller's remorse, so I refused to accept these conditions and told Mr. Poffenberg to return the deposit. They then changed the contract back to the terms of my original counteroffer and signed it. I had learned when I was in the business that you must accept an offer with no conditions if you want a binding contract. Any change, however small, serves to reject the proposal and change it into a counteroffer. The other party then has the option of accepting or refusing it. I told Poffenberg I rejected the buyers' counteroffer and had no desire to continue the negotiations. I directed him to return the earnest money deposit and to tell the buyers the deal was dead.

I had no formal listing agreement with Poffenberg, so he had no claim for a commission, absent an actual sale. He returned the deposit and told the buyers they didn't have a leg to stand on. The buyers were most unhappy, but Poffenberg was philosophical about losing the sale. He had not advertised it and had spent very little time on the negotiations. I think he disliked the lawyer and blamed him for killing the deal because he couldn't let well enough alone.

Some time later I was talking to Mr. Poffenberg and mentioned that I had to be careful doing business in Florida, since I had the disadvantage of being a hillbilly from Tennessee. He said maybe so, but I was about the swiftest hillbilly he ever hoped to see. Coming from him that was a compliment. A few years later, I sold the building for almost twice what my counteroffer had been.

Management Makes
The Difference

LESSON 24: Raise your rents more frequently and in smaller increments, rather than big raises less often. Give plenty of advance notice of coming increases, so the tenants have time to get used to the idea before having to pay the increases. They will be less likely to give notice impulsively and then regret it later.

LESSON 25: Always get estoppel letters from all tenants when buying rental property. Make your contract contingent on getting these letters prior to settlement to verify the information the seller has given you.

The previous owner of the Broward County 30-unit building had an arrangement with one of the tenants, a Mrs. Wickham. He deducted $100 from her monthly rent in return for her showing vacant apartments and taking the rent payments the first of each month. Her son, Brooks, had Down's syndrome. I continued this arrangement for a year or more until her brother died and she moved in with his widow. She told me once she had a rental application from an attractive woman of another race. She said she got rid of her by telling her she might not fit in with the other tenants, who were all white at the time. I had warned her before about discrimination, but obviously I had not made it plain enough. I didn't sleep very well for a few nights because I was afraid the woman might have been a tester from the Equal Opportunity Commission. We both could have been in trouble, and I made sure she never did that again.

I originally had one-year leases, but eventually I added the condition that either party could cancel without penalty by giving 30 days written notice to the other. I did this because I always released tenants from their leases when they gave me hard-luck stories. I never wanted an unhappy tenant who would rather be living somewhere else. Also, when market conditions changed enough to justify higher rents, I did not want to wait several months for leases to expire. I still had written leases, however, in order to define the rights of both parties.

♠ ♠ ♠ ♠

When an apartment building is sold, the seller should get a letter from each tenant as to the term of the lease, the amount of the rent, the advance rent paid if any, and the amount of the security deposit. The buyer should insist on having those letters before settlement, otherwise he may find himself stuck with long-term leases on one or more apartments at half the usual rent. Or they could be sweetheart deals for close relatives or friends of the previous owner, and they could have options to renew for the next 10 years at the same rent. These letters will estop (prevent) the tenants from making some such claim later. That's why they are called estoppel letters. Neither a lawyer's opinion of title nor a title insurance policy will protect you from the rights of persons in possession of the premises (tenants) or from such encroachments as a survey might reveal. Title companies always put these disclaimers in their title policies and their interim binders. This is especially important in commercial transactions, as we will discuss later.

♠ ♠ ♠ ♠

In the mid-1970s, I bought a new 4-unit apartment building in Florida in the community of Lauderdale Lakes. The price was right, and one of the apartments had already been leased. I knew the lease was for one year and I knew what the monthly rent was, but I did not read the lease. After I took possession, I found that the lease allowed the tenant to keep a German shepherd dog in the apartment. Not long later, I learned they kept the dog locked up in the living room for about 10 hours every work day. At the end of their lease I asked them to move. I then got professional cleaners to come in and try to get rid of the stains and the odors in the carpet. Their best efforts failed and I finally had to remove the carpet and take it to the garbage dump. My wife and I love dogs, and we have two that live in our home now. But they are house broken and we don't leave them alone and unattended for 10 hours at a time.

We sold that building after a couple of years and took our profit in the form of a second mortgage. The buyer was Tony Laurie, an agent for the Keyes Real Estate Company, the biggest in Florida at the time. When we were divorced, I got that note and mortgage as part of a very amicable property settlement. After I took the job in Washington and had additional income, I signed the note over and assigned the mortgage to my former wife. Tony offered to pay off the note for a small discount, and she accepted. The kids were adults and gone by then, so she used the money for a down payment on a town house and rented out the main home we had lived in.

We had a period of gradually increasing rents for several years, and I tried to keep up with the market rates. I found the tenants accepted small increases each year more willingly than they did larger increases less frequently. I also learned to give tenants two months advance notice of rent increases. That gave them a month to think about it before having to give me 30 days notice if they thought they would move rather than pay the higher rent. The tenants were then less likely to make an impulsive decision to move and regret it later.

♠ ♠ ♠ ♠

I was never mechanically inclined, but I had to learn a few things to survive. After paying a service man a few times to come and blow out an air conditioner drain line, I bought a little bottle of compressed carbon dioxide and started blowing out those lines myself. I eventually learned that some chlorine bleach in the pan where the condensed water collects will help prevent algae from clogging the drain lines and causing leaks from overflows.

We had a do-it-yourself plumbing shop nearby, and they were good about giving free advice with the parts they sold. I soon learned to replace a washer in a faucet to stop it from dripping and to remove and clean, or replace, the water trap under a sink. The 12-unit building had garbage disposals in the kitchens and I even replaced a few of them at first. But the other building did not have disposals and the tenants didn't seem to mind. I finally started taking them out and not replacing them when they failed. The kitchen stoves had heating elements in the ovens that plugged in; so when one went bad, I just bought a new one and replaced it myself.

I bought 30 dead-bolt locks, all keyed separately, and had two master keys made for myself that would open them all. I did not go in without the tenant there except by prior arrangement or in an emergency. I bought an electric drill and a bit that cut a round hole the size of the locks. Working slowly and carefully, I installed one of those locks in each of the front doors. In addition, I installed a little peephole gadget in each front door so the tenant could see who rang the doorbell before opening the door.

I arranged with the Glidden Paint Company to supply all the paint for inside painting. I used only latex paint and only in oyster white. The walls, ceiling, and trim all got the same. Between tenants, washing the walls and a little touch up with paint was usually sufficient, and a full paint job on an empty apartment went fast. I once agreed to paint an occupied apartment for a good tenant who had been there several years. She had many pictures hanging on the walls that had to be removed and replaced, and she had her place stuffed with furniture. It was a miserable chore, and I never did that again. Thereafter, I told the tenants I would provide the paint but they would have to do the work.

I cleaned the pool at least twice a week, adding chlorine as necessary and muriatic acid or other products to keep the pH level within proper limits. The filters in the pump house had to be changed from time to time, and I usually did that myself. After a few years, we drained the pool and refinished the inside with Marsite. The deck around the pool was light brown and finished with tiny pebbles to guard against it becoming too slippery. Eventually it started to crack and sink in places, and I had to have it reinforced. The contractor drilled about 20 holes through the surface of the deck and into the ground and pumped in a cement mixture under pressure. That solved the problem.

We were connected to the Wilton Manors sewer system, and we had a well with an electric pump to provide water for the lawn. That saved money two ways, since the sewer bill was based partially on the amount of our water bill. I had an automatic sprinkler system installed with a timer to regulate the watering. I bought a power lawn mower for the property and did the mowing myself. I stored it in a shed next to the pump house by the pool.

All the apartments had wall-to-wall carpets, and some of them eventually had to be replaced. I never tried to repair or replace them myself, although my son David installed two or three. I usually got a professional to put in new carpets of what they called FHA quality, which is the minimum grade FHA will approve in a house where they insure the loan.

The cost of the garbage collection in Wilton Manors was high and I looked around for another garbage company to do it. I learned that any company could operate in Wilton Manors if they paid the city a license fee of $14,000 a year. Wilton Manors is not very big, so no company could afford to pay that fee unless they got all the business. That kept out any new companies that wanted to compete and the one with the monopoly could charge high prices.

My sister, Eunice, at age 13 with twin brothers, Billie and Bobbie. The twins were premature and both had cerebral palsey from birth, no doubt from injury during the delivery at home. Our mother died of typhoid fever when the twins were three years old, and Eunice as the only girl in the family missed two years of high school in order to stay home and minister to them. Eunice has two daughters, Judy Baggett and Janice Pannell. (photo courtesy of Eunice White Curtis)

Absentee Ownership Makes Problems

I was divorced in August 1978. In December of that year I was invited to move to Washington, D.C. to work as executive assistant to an old friend, the recently elected CEO of a not-for-profit association. It was a no-fault divorce and an amicable property settlement. My spouse got the house and furniture, the savings account, and a substantial percentage of my retirement annuity for as long as we both lived. I got sole ownership of the 30 apartments and a second mortgage on a little four unit we had sold. I left my second son, David, in charge of the apartments. He managed them for about a year and then went to Georgia Tech to study Electrical Engineering.

♠ ♠ ♠ ♠

I went back to Florida for a few days and ran a classified ad for a person or a couple to manage the Broward County 30-unit building in return for free rent. I had about 30 calls on the ad, and I hired Tom and Cheryl Hurd for the job. Cheryl had a full-time job, but she kept the books, handled the bank deposits, and made monthly reports to me. They kept a small cash fund for incidentals. As they spent money from it, they sent me receipts. When the fund got low I sent a check to replace what they had spent. I wrote all the checks from Washington for mortgage payments and for all bills of any significance. Tom was around during the day, so he showed the apartments and took care of minor problems. If he had to paint an apartment or do any other major repair, I paid him extra.

When I had to replace some air conditioner compressors, I noticed they were usually the ones that served the upstairs apartments. The downstairs units were cooler because they had the upstairs apartments between them and the sun. I installed several spinner ventilators on the roof to help expel the heated air from the attic and this helped. It also helped when I installed tinted film that reflected the sun's rays on all the upstairs windows that faced the afternoon sun.

Both buildings had asphalt shingle roofs that after a few years got ugly and dirty looking from mildew or mold. We also started having leaks from time to time. So when I refinanced the second mortgage in early 1982, I had the roofs replaced. Tom Hurd solicited the bids and supervised the work. We stripped off the old roof, put down heavy-duty underlay, and installed light gray, mildew-resistant fiberglass shingles. Tom made sure they did a good job, and the place looked wonderful after it was done. I'm sure the new roof helped when I sold the property a couple of years later.

The new roof cost me $17,000 and I couldn't count it as an expense for tax purposes. I had to count it as a capital improvement and depreciate it over its estimated useful life. If it had been a roof repair costing a few hundred dollars, I could have deducted it from that year's income for tax purposes. A new roof had to be capitalized and added to my tax basis in the property. That would help to reduce my capital gain when I sold it.

I did not keep a separate bank account for security deposits and advance rents. I elected instead to pay the tenants 5 percent interest on those funds. The Florida law required me to do that if I did not keep the money in a separate account. When I received a security deposit I had to report it as income, and when I refunded a security deposit I reported it as an expense. That eventually caused me to have a tax problem. In 1981 we rarely had vacancies and rents were going up. Tom saw this as a good opportunity to make new tenants pay the first and last month's rent plus a security deposit equal to one month's rent. That was equal to three months' rent to move in, and it was all taxable income.

♠ ♠ ♠ ♠

I had met Linda in July 1981 and we were planning to marry in June 1982. I did not have my tax return ready by the regular filing date, so I filed for an automatic extension until June 15 and sent an estimated payment. We had to be sure and return from the first stage of our honeymoon by that date, because I had to go to the office of my CPA, pick up the tax return, and mail it before midnight that night. When I got there, I found I owed many thousands of dollars more. I mailed the check and then scurried around the next day and got enough cash in the checking account to cover it. Luckily, I had it from the refinancing of the second mortgage.

An early photo of my wife Linda and her sisters, brother, and aunt. Shown here are Martha (now Tappan) in front and (l-r) Linda, Julie (now Wood), Harvey Coleman, and their aunt, Miss Jane Ryon. (photo courtesy of Linda White)

Continuing Formal Real-Estate Education

When I left Florida in 1953 to enter the Border Patrol, I changed my broker license to inactive status. Since I moved several times, I used the home of my mother-in -law as my permanent address in Florida. It cost one dollar a year for inactive status, and I could reactivate it at my convenience by paying the fee. I kept my license inactive for 21 years. When I retired in Miami in 1974, I was back in business the next day as a broker-salesman. They changed the law later and that is no longer possible.

We were living in nearby Hollywood when I was working in Miami, and we continued to live there after I retired. I worked first for Klock Realty. The owner, Joe Klock, was a nationally known motivational speaker on the subject of real estate and on selling in general. He was very charismatic and could have been a successful television evangelist if he had taken that direction. His son, Joe Klock, Jr., is a prominent lawyer in Florida, and he played a visible part in the court proceedings concerning the 2000 election there.

Mr. Klock insisted that I sell only houses, so I soon moved to Prestige Realty and specialized in commercial properties. There I went into the Certified Commercial Investment Member (CCIM) program sponsored by the National Association of Real Estate Boards (NAREB). The name of the organization has since been changed. That was the nearest thing there was to a doctorate in the commercial real-estate field.

♣ ♣ ♣ ♣

A candidate had to first complete five courses of academic study. Each of the courses lasted a week, Monday through Friday, and there was a three-hour written examination on Saturday. We had eight hours of instruction each day and then two hours for dinner. We came back for a supervised study period from 7 p.m. to 9 p.m. An extra hour was optional, and most of us stayed for that also.

Of the five courses, only one location was within commuting distance and that was in North Miami. The others were Atlanta, Orlando, and two in the Washington, D.C. area. The tuition alone for each course was about $400, not to mention the additional costs for transportation, food, and lodging. The grading was strict, and anyone who did not pass had to repeat the course. Each candidate also had to complete a specified number of commercial transactions and write a demonstration report on one of them. This report had to describe the transaction and explain how the candidate had used the principles of the courses. The instructors supervised and monitored each demonstration report as if it were a thesis or dissertation at a university.

I passed all the academic courses and did a limited partnership transaction that would have served for my demonstration report. I never got the designation, however, because I went inactive and moved to the Washington, D.C. area after I was divorced.

Between CCIM courses I attended a Realtors Institute session in nearby Boca Raton and earned the designation GRI (Graduate of the Realtors Institute.) I also took a course in appraising property.

Syndications And Limited Partnerships

LESSON 26: Few sales happen by themselves. Be flexible and make it as easy as possible on the principals.

LESSON 27: Be careful what you say in responding to a credit reference. Keep it simple and factually accurate.

Before leaving Florida, I took a course in syndications taught by Carleton Sheets (the same one who has been on nation-wide TV in recent years selling his program for making money in a hurry in real estate). Syndication was a hot subject in those days, and this course helped me with one of my own investments. My sales record was only so-so during those years in Hollywood. I sold several properties, but I spent much of my time taking courses and looking after my investment with the 30 units.

The manager of the commercial office of Prestige Realty arranged for the commercial salesmen to pay a certain amount of money each month toward the operation of the office and to pay for their own advertising. That covered the overhead for the office, and the broker then took only 10 percent of the sales commissions instead of the usual 50 percent.

He also had a residential sales section in the same office that operated in the usual manner. The residential people were not allowed to do commercial deals except in cooperation with a commercial agent and vice versa. He argued that a brain surgeon shouldn't attempt to do a heart transplant procedure and vice versa;

and a man on trial for murder shouldn't have a divorce lawyer for his defense attorney. Accordingly, real estate agents can serve their customers better if they specialize. As the old saying goes, "A jack-of-all-trades is master of none."

♠ ♠ ♠ ♠

Meanwhile, I found a fairly new 10-unit building not far from the Fort Lauderdale Airport. It had been listed but had not sold, and the listing had expired without being renewed. Two 5-unit buildings faced each other, about 40 feet apart. The lot was deeper than it was wide, and it continued back to a lake about 150 feet away. Several trees added to the scenic value of the property. The backs of the two buildings were parallel to the sidelines of the lot.

Each apartment had two bedrooms, one bath, a living room, a kitchen, and a dinette with wooden paneling. A construction company had built four of these complexes, all from the same plan. The owner had been the bookkeeper for the company, and he bought this one when the company went out of business. He and his wife had owned it three years but had recently run into trouble. Someone had called the owner about a credit reference for a former tenant. The owner had said the tenant was a deadbeat and a liar and not to be trusted. The former tenant then filed a lawsuit against the owner for slander. These complications convinced the owners they did not want to be landlords, so they agreed to sell the property to me and to pay a 6 percent sales commission to my broker.

I talked to some friends who had money to invest and arranged for three of them to participate. The four of us would put equal amounts into the limited partnership. I would make a sales commission on the purchase, and on the eventual sale upon disposition.

We agreed to make a down payment and assume the two first mortgages, one on each five-unit building, and to give the sellers two second mortgages, one on each building. This would leave the partnership enough money for legal fees and an adequate operating fund. I would be the general partner and assume all liability. I would also make all decisions except as to any refinancing, which would be by agreement among the partners. The limited partners would have no liability other than their initial investment.

The general partner is expected to have the expertise to make the investment work and to assume liability in case something goes wrong. The limited partners must be passive investors and are not allowed to participate in operating decisions. That would put the partnership in jeopardy of being classified by IRS as a corporation and subject to double taxation.

A limited partnership pays no taxes at the partnership level, and depreciation losses are passed through to the partners. But calling it a limited partnership is not enough. Unless it meets certain strict guidelines, IRS will consider it a corporation and tax it accordingly. They told us in syndication classes that you cannot hang a sign on a cow and change it into a horse.

I was to manage the property with no extra compensation, and I was to pay each partner 9 percent a year on his investment from the cash flow, payable monthly. Since I owned a full share, I paid myself the same.

The down payment was to be held in escrow by my broker and to be returned if the sale did not close, so my broker advanced me my share. My share of the commission from the seller was just enough to cover my investment in the limited partnership. I got a lawyer who was familiar with such things to draw up the limited partnership agreement and we wrote the contract for sale.

The sellers would not sign the contract without a condition that they find a suitable house to buy. They finally settled on one listed by one of our residential agents, and that agent and I wrote an offer on that house. The apartment sellers wanted the purchase contingent on the closing of the sale of the apartments but the house sellers did not agree to that. They were giving a good deal with a low down payment, and they wanted no uncertainty about the sale going to closing.

I finally had to write a backup contract to buy the house myself at the same price and terms in case the apartment owners did not complete their purchase. Everything was resolved eventually. All three contracts were signed (including my backup) and both sales were closed and the deeds recorded. We then tore up my backup contract. I breathed easily at last and hosted a wine and cheese party after work for the other agents in the office.

♠ ♠ ♠ ♠

The partnership owned the property about 18 months and then sold it. We had not offered it for sale, but an agent came to me and wanted to buy it. I had some concern about the proximity to the very busy Fort Lauderdale Airport, so we worked out an acceptable contract of sale. The agreed upon commission was 3.3 percent. The selling broker got the customary 3 percent and my broker got 3/10 of 1 percent, which is 10 percent of 3 percent. That was his full share of a normal commission under our working arrangement. I took no commission on the sale. Each partner got 9 percent interest a year during the holding period plus a profit of 35 percent when we sold, a total return of 48 percent in 18 months. Since I got a full share of the proceeds, I thought it would be too greedy of me to also take a commission on the sale.

When word got around about the outcome of that investment, I had people calling me for a similar deal. The problem was finding another property that offered a similar opportunity for profit. Limited partnerships got a bad name because so many bought buildings for tax shelters rather than for their value as investments. A syndicator can get into trouble when the asset is not an economic success. I would not syndicate anything that I would not be willing to buy with my own money if I could afford it. I never found another such property. Not long thereafter, I put my license into inactive status and moved to Washington D.C. to work.

A few years later the buyers told me the Fort Lauderdale Airport expansion and a new runway put low-flying planes directly over these apartments. The airport authority accordingly took the property by eminent domain. They had a lawsuit over the fair market value that had to be paid to the owners, and I never learned what happened.

♠ ♠ ♠ ♠

Cynics say a syndication is a working arrangement for investment wherein the investors have the money and the general partner has the experience. Then after the investment has run its course and they cash out, the general partner has the money and the investors have the experience. My limited partners were happy, but many syndications don't end that way. When the general partners are so caught up on tax deductions that they pay twice the real value for properties to syndicate, that is a recipe for disaster.

(top) Robert A. Tappan and wife Joan with three children in 1999. Left to right are Sam, Hannah, and Molly. (bottom) Four Tappan children, Christmas 2001. Left to right are Hannah, Molly, and a later arrival, Ellie. Sam is in front. Robert is a graduate of Georgetown University and is currently Deputy Assistant Secretary of State for Public Affairs. Joan works as a project manager for Boeing Aircraft. She attended Skidmore, in Saratoga Springs, N.Y., for two years, then took off for a year-and-a-half to ride young horses at a thoroughbred farm, helping to prepare them for racing. She later finished her degree at Rutgers. She and Robert met when they both worked for the Republican National Committee during the administration of the first President Bush. (photos courtesy of Robert A. Tappan)

Investment Property Brokerage

LESSON 28: Do not believe everything you are told when looking at investment property. Read all the leases and evaluate all the details. Make sure the rents being paid are not inflated to boost the apparent value of the real estate. Watch out for long-term options for renewals.

LESSON 29: The lower the Cap Rate, the higher the value. The higher the Cap Rate, the lower the value. An appraiser can make a dramatic difference in the estimated value of a property simply by assuming a different Cap Rate.

During this period a man came to me and wanted to sell an office building in Hallandale, Florida. He was one of the investors in a limited partnership that had built the building a few years previously. I thought it was unusual, because such a sale would normally be handled by the general partner and not by one of the limited partners. He gave me the income and expense figures, but I insisted on seeing the actual leases for all the tenants.

The building did not have separate electric meters for the individual offices and so the rents included all utilities. The air conditioning and the heating were both electric and the bills were high. Electric rates had doubled during the previous three or four years and the cost had reduced the profits of the building. The general partners (two lawyers) occupied about 20 percent of the space in the entire building, and they had a favorable location in the building and a favorable price on their rent, even without the free utilities. The man who talked to me said I should not worry about that because all the leases would expire in about two years and the rents could be adjusted. I read all the leases and learned that the general partners had given themselves the option of renewing their lease for four more five-year terms at the same rent. The only adjustment was a pro-rata share of any additional taxes on the building. None of the other leases had the option for this 20-year extension, just the one the general partners put in for themselves.

They naturally were happy with their sweetheart deal, but the limited partners were trying to get out of a bad situation. I told the man I had no hope of selling the building for anything near what he wanted. Also, the general partners would have to negotiate any sale of the building, and he would have a very difficult time if he tried to sell his limited-partner share to someone else. I think he may have had cause for a lawsuit against the general partners, but it was not my place to suggest it.

♠ ♠ ♠ ♠

A reverse situation involved a small medical building that was for sale, also in Hallandale, Florida. Six doctors had formed a general partnership (all six equally responsible and liable) and built a medical clinic. Then the partnership rented the suites to the individual doctors. It was a three-floor building with an elevator, and there were two suites on each floor. The doctors all had leases that were to expire in two years, and all had options for renewal. The renewals could be for two more five-year terms at the present rent plus a cost of living increase based on the consumer's price index.

In my CCIM studies I had learned to be careful in any situation where a tenant is paying rent to himself. I did a market survey and learned that the doctors were paying themselves approximately $100 a month more in rent per unit than the average tenant would have paid at that time for the same space. The higher rent was a direct cost of doing business for the doctors and was fully deductible from ordinary income for tax purposes. At the same time, the extra income to the partnership from the higher rent was partially sheltered by the depreciation IRS allowed on the building each year.

For purposes of a sale, the building then showed an artificially inflated net operating income, which is a big factor in determining the market value of the property. An appraiser calculates how much income is left after paying all operating expenses. These expenses include maintenance, repairs, taxes, and insurance, to name a few. It does not include debt service, which is annual mortgage payments of principal and interest.

What is left is called the net operating income, or the NOI for short. To estimate market value a capitalization (cap) rate is assigned, and this Cap Rate depends on the element of risk in the investment. For example, a fairly new apartment building in a premium location with long-term tenants might sell for a Cap Rate of 8 percent at that time. In other words, an investor might be willing to accept a return of 8 percent on his money for such a high-quality investment. But an old run-down building in a poor neighborhood with transient tenants might demand a return of 12 percent or more because of the greater risk of the investment and the expected problems of management.

The location was not the greatest, so the doctors set their price for the building based on a Cap Rate of 10 percent. (For example, a net operating income of $20,000 with a Cap Rate of 10 would indicate a market value of $200,000.)

The formula is referred to as I/RV (I divided by R times V), where I =NOI, R=rate (or Cap Rate), and V= value, or fair market value. If any two of these factors are known, using this formula can solve for the unknown factor. In other words:

> If the NOI is $20,000 and the Cap Rate is 10 percent, the value is $200,000. (Divide the NOI by the Cap Rate to get the value. Use the decimal form of the percentage.)

Given the same $20,000 NOI, a Cap Rate of 12 percent would indicate a market value of $166,667, while a Cap Rate of 8 percent would indicate a market value of $250,000.

$20,000 divided by .12 indicates a market value of $166, 667
$20,000 divided by .08 equals a market value of $250,000.

$250,000 (value) times Cap Rate (.08) equals the NOI, $20,000
$20,000 NOI divided by the value ($250,000) equals the Cap Rate (.08), of 8 percent.

But the six doctors, each paying $100 a month more than the market value of the space, produced an artificial excess of $7,200 a year in net operating income. Since the doctors had set their asking price based on a reasonable Cap Rate of 10 percent, that meant they were asking $72,000 more than the building was worth at the prevailing market for similar space. In other words, if a buyer had to replace the doctors with all new tenants paying the normal market rents, the net income would be $7,200 less than what they were showing, and the building would be worth $72,000 less.

Just to make sure I was not being unfair I asked the doctor who was offering the building for sale if he was going to exercise the option to renew his lease when it expired. He would not give me a direct answer; so I asked him about the other doctors in the building, and he was still evasive. He finally admitted they were planning to build another clinic on a piece of land they had already bought. No doubt they planned to set up a similar arrangement with the new building. I crossed that building off my list. If somebody bought it, the doctors would not renew those leases and the inflated market value of the building would drop by about $72,000 two years later.

♠ ♠ ♠ ♠

It is not unusual, however, for an owner-operator to sell a building and lease it back on a long-term lease A business normally pays a greater return on invested capital than real estate pays, because running a business requires more intensive management than owning real estate. Often the sale and leaseback is an arms-length transaction beneficial to both parties. The buyer of the real estate gets a long-term tenant and a reasonable return on his investment. He also gets tax deductions from depreciation, while the seller gets cash he can use to expand his business where he can earn a higher return on his money.

♠ ♠ ♠ ♠

In 1982, after I married again and resigned my position with the association, I got a real estate license in Maryland. I still hoped to form another limited partnership if I could find a good property. Research in the public records turned up a strip shopping center the owner was willing to sell. A bank building was at one end and a Safeway supermarket was at the other. A few other small stores filled the space between them. The owner and his wife had built the center in the mid-1960s, about 20 years previously, but they had recently divorced and wanted to liquidate. They were asking $2 million and said they wouldn't take less than $1.5 million. But the Safeway store occupied about 30,000 square feet and the lease was still at $2 a square foot a year. That came to $60,000 a year, but the normal rental for that space at the time should have been about $4 a square foot, or $120,000 a year.

The owner told me not to worry about that because Safeway was going to close that store the next year. Safeway was then building stores with 50,000 square feet, and a store as small as this one was no longer economically feasible. The owners planned to at least double the rent from that space when Safeway moved. I made some calls and talked to the manager of properties for the Safeway Corporation. He confirmed they did plan to close that store, but they had no intention of giving up the lease. He said the original lease was for $2 per square foot per year, and the options for renewals added up to 49 years. There were no provisions for increasing rents except in case of increased taxes or increased cost for maintenance of the parking areas. He said when they closed the store they would sublease the space for at least twice what they would be paying the owners.

He said Safeway did this with most of its stores, and they made about as much in the long run on their real estate as they did operating their grocery stores. I asked him why anyone would sign such a lease. He said $2 a square foot was a generous rent when they built the building, and without the Safeway lease already signed, the owner could not have obtained the financing to build the center. The owner did not have much choice in the matter. In addition, most owners thought Safeway did not renew their leases when they closed stores. We now have the benefit of 20-20 hindsight, but in the mid-1960s there was not much concern about problems with rising interest rates and inflation in the future.

I could not recommend that property because the owner was telling people things about Safeway's plans that I knew to be false. The truth would come out in the end, and I would look like either a fool or a crook. The store closed a year later and Safeway subleased the space to a Highs store, a chili parlor, and a beauty salon. The center eventually sold for a million dollars, according to public records. Without that long-term Safeway lease it probably would have sold for a half-million more.

♣ ♣ ♣ ♣

There was an additional aspect to the Safeway deal. In any shopping center, large or small, anchor stores are necessary to draw traffic. In this case the Safeway supermarket was the only anchor. In a large, regional shopping center, department stores such as Sears Roebuck, Lord & Taylor, or J. C. Penny are the anchors, and there are usually three or four of them. They are called generators because they generate traffic for the smaller stores and shops in the center. A small key shop in a mall might pay 20 or more times the rent per square foot that a big department store pays. They can afford to pay high rent per square foot because their space is small and the department stores bring a steady stream of traffic through the mall, providing customers for the small shops.

In a strip shopping center the generator is usually a supermarket, a major drug store, or both. When the Safeway store closed, the center had no generator and so the traffic fell off and the other businesses suffered. If Safeway had agreed to terminate their lease, or if they had allowed somebody else to buy the remaining portion of their lease, it might have been possible to get another supermarket in the space. Some independent supermarkets would not have demanded any more room than was available there and would have been glad to lease the space.

But Safeway elected to divide the space and lease to three smaller stores or shops, and this left the center without a generator. When the leases expire for the other smaller shops, the owners of the real estate may have to reduce the rent because there is no supermarket there to draw traffic. Safeway has no problem because their long-term lease is at such a low rental they can sublease the space and make more than a million dollars profit by the time the lease expires in another 20-something years.

My wife, Linda, with our grandson, John Joseph, at his first
Easter. Linda's aunt, the late Miss Jane Ryon, is also shown. She
was born in 1910 and worked for many years for the Board of
Immigration Appeals. She was also a member of the Watergate
Jury and is a sweet lady loved by all who know her. (photo by
Stephen W. White)

Mixing Residential And Commercial Sales

LESSON 30: Be careful about what you wish for, because you might get it and be sorry you did.

LESSON 31: There are plenty of buyers for good properties if the price is right. The problem is finding sellers who have something good to sell at the going market price.

LESSON 32: Don't count your chickens before they hatch. "There's many a slip between the cup and the lip," as they say. Wait until the check clears before you spend the commission money or boast about the deal.

Occasionally, when I was concentrating on commercial and investment properties, a residential agent asked me to cooperate on a sale because he had a customer who wanted to buy an apartment building or a warehouse. According to the agent, his customer usually had a lot of money and wanted to buy right away. The residential agent always expected to divide the commission 50-50 with the agent producing the buyer, while I found the property.

Once a residential agent came to me in Florida and said he had a customer who wanted to buy 20 to 40 apartment units not more than 10 years old. They all had to be two-bedroom units, preferably with 1-1/2 baths each. They had to be located on a canal with ocean access, east of Federal Highway in Broward County, and could not cost more than $17,000 a unit. The agent who related this to me was excited because he thought he was going to be involved in a big commercial sale. I had to tell him I already knew investors who would buy that in a minute if such a property existed at that price.

The best residential agent rarely understands all the complexities of a large commercial transaction, and the best commercial agent usually does not understand all the complexities of a residential sale. If a man needs a doctor or a lawyer, he would be well advised to find one who specializes in whatever he needs done at the time. Why shouldn't it be the same with real estate?

♠ ♠ ♠ ♠

In the middle 1980s, I decided to specialize in apartment buildings in Maryland and nearby Virginia. I did research and compiled lists of apartment buildings in the various areas. I found there were many buildings in Takoma Park, Maryland, and I did a mailing to contact all the owners I could identify. One response came from the owner of a 33-unit building there. The owner had listed it in the multiple-listing service a few months previously, but had later taken it off the market and told everybody it was no longer for sale. He called me and said he would still sell it if we could work out a private sale without everybody knowing about it. He would not sign an exclusive listing because he said he did that before and he did not want to deal with so many people coming around to bother him. He agreed to sell for a substantial reduction from the original listing price. Takoma Park had rent control at the time, and that helped hold down the price of apartment buildings there. I knew one investor who might be interested because he had other units nearby. I called him but learned he would be out of town for 10 days.

One man in the office had been after me to find an apartment building for his "personal friend who had plenty of money and wanted to invest it." I finally decided I should not be greedy, so I prepared a fact sheet for him and agreed to show the property to his customer at 10:00 a.m. the next day. When we were getting ready to go pick up the customers, the other agent said they were going to meet us at the property. I told him that was a no-no, but the deed was already done. When we got there at the appointed time, they had been there an hour earlier and were already gone. The owner was upset because they had come in like bulls in a china shop and showed him no courtesy at all.

They finally made a low offer. I got the owner to make a reasonable counteroffer, but the buyers held it three or four days without giving us an answer. At the same time, the other agent was on the phone talking to friends in the real-estate office where he previously worked, boasting about his big deal. Within a day, an agent in that other office sold the building to another buyer. I asked him why his old office had happened to sell this building when it was not on the market and right when we were working on it.

"I told them I was working on a hot deal for a 33-unit building in Takoma Park," he admitted, "but I didn't tell them where it was."

"Every active commercial agent in town knows there is only one 33-unit building in Takoma Park," I replied, "and any salesman worth his salt can find out the name and address of the owner in 20 minutes. But nobody else knew the owner was willing to sell it, until you started boasting about your big deal. Maybe this will teach you to hold your tongue until you cash your commission check!"

♠ ♠ ♠ ♠

Later, I got another response concerning a 35-unit building in Gaithersburg, Maryland. It was owned by a man who was 84 years old and wanted to sell it. I submitted an offer in partnership with a professional man who wanted a tax shelter. We made him a good offer, with a 6 percent commission to my broker. My share of the down payment was to come from my sales commission. We planned to have a limited partnership similar to the one I did in Florida several years previously. I would be the general partner, manage the property, and have over-all financial responsibility. The owner was to hold a first mortgage, since there was no mortgage on it at the time.

The owner said the contract was satisfactory, but he wanted his lawyer to look at it before he signed it. His 50-year-old son did not want his father to sell, because he wanted to inherit it eventually. The son already owned a smaller building nearby that his father had built for him a few years previously. After two or three days the owner called me and said his lawyer would not let him sign the contract.

The lawyer had said if his heirs inherited the building when he died, there would be no capital-gains tax to pay if he then sold it. There would be a step-up in tax basis to the appraised value as of the time of death. If he sold the property instead and the heirs inherited the mortgage, the heirs would have the same tax basis in the mortgage that the father had, and he would have to pay taxes on the profits as he received them in the monthly mortgage payments. There would be no step-up in tax basis for a mortgage. Since the owner built the building himself several years ago and had been taking depreciation, his tax basis was very low.

The lawyer said the contract was fair enough, but from an estate-planning standpoint he could not let his client sign it. I had been told by one of my CCIM instructors that there was a step-up basis in a mortgage you inherit, just as in real property. Therefore, I didn't believe the lawyer and I did some research to try to prove him wrong. I had a friend who worked at one of the tax-advisory services in D.C. and they allowed me to use their library one afternoon. I finally had to admit he was right and I was wrong.

I have no quarrel with the lawyer who killed that deal. He gave legal advice concerning tax implications, but he didn't substitute his real estate judgment for that of the seller. As it turned out, he did me a favor without knowing it. Soon thereafter, the tax reform act of 1986 was signed into law and many of the tax advantages of real estate were taken away. As a result, the market value of most investment properties dropped suddenly by about 20 percent. That's when I went inactive as an agent.

♠ ♠ ♠ ♠

The company I was associated with, Long & Foster, had a good training program, and I heard a couple of interesting stories there about commercial ventures. The first one was about the hill and the hole. One man owned a well located plot, but the ground was too high to build on. Another man owned the plot next to it, but it was a big sinkhole and was unsuitable for building. So they formed a partnership with a man who had an earth-moving company. He used his equipment to move the hill into the hole and make both plots level. Then the three of them owned equal shares in a desirable property. That may not have been a true story, but it does illustrate a concept.

We were assured another story was true. There was a well-located plot of several acres near a large city in the South, but the elevation was so high it was not suitable for building. Then the word got out that a highway would be built nearby the next year. One entrepreneur found out where the road would go and discovered they would need a tremendous amount of fill dirt for one long section of the road. So he bought an option on the unsuitable land. He paid a cash amount for the right to buy it at a specific price for a certain period of time. His only risk was the cash he paid for the option. Then he went to the road building company and made a deal for them to use their earth-moving equipment to get all their fill dirt from his property at so much a cubic yard. He ended up owning a highly desirable, level property, improved and paid for by the sale of the fill dirt. There is now a regional shopping center on that land, and he is in Florida, living a life of ease on Longboat Key.

My daughter, Melissa S. White, as a young adult.
She has two B.A. degrees, one in philosophy from
the University of South Florida, and one in English
from San Francisco State University. She also has
an M.F.A. in writing from Mills College. After
finishing her education, she taught writing and
English as a Second Language at various schools,
including two colleges in Kyoto, Japan. She entered
the non-profit sector upon returning to San
Francisco and worked for the International Institute
of the East Bay and Breast Cancer Action. In 2001
she started her own small business, Dachshund
Development, as a fund-raising consultant
specializing in grant writing. She and her partner,
Tracy, have two cats and hope to get a dachshund
puppy one day. (photo courtesy of Melissa S.
White)

Beware Of Get-Rich-Quick Schemes

LESSON 33: Be skeptical of the claim that there is a way to gain wealth rapidly and easily in real estate by using some "system" for a few hours a week in your spare time.

LESSON 34: The nothing down technique works best when real estate prices are rising constantly. There will be serious dips from time to time and the "nothing down" artists can be wiped out.

LESSON 35: If you buy lottery tickets, buy them for fun and use money that you don't really need. Do not use your rent money or your grocery money. The odds against you are overwhelming, and nothing is more useless than last week's losing lottery tickets.

If you are looking for a quick and easy way to get rich, don't waste your time reading this book. But if you want a realistic look at the world of real estate, this book is for you. They pre-empted the phrase "The good, the bad, and the ugly" for the Clint Eastwood movie, but those words would apply equally to the real estate business.

In recent years the airwaves and cyberspace have been cluttered with pie-in-the-sky schemes for getting rich in real estate in a very short time. Honest-looking and earnest-sounding people of all kinds appear in some of these ads. They look you right in the eye and tell you they were broke, in debt, and with bad credit until they bought the book, or the cassettes, or the secret formula being advertised. And lo and behold, within three months (and in their spare time) they had an income of $10,000 or more a month from their real estate investments, all bought with OPM (other peoples money.) Also, when these "students" talk about their million dollars of net worth after about a year of using this system, I remember the little boy who said he sold his dog for $1,000. When pressed, he admitted that he had been paid with two $500 cats.

♠ ♠ ♠ ♠

I borrowed Robert Allen's book, *Nothing Down*, from the library and read some of it. Allen is a talented writer and his book has sold a gazillion copies. I would not quarrel with some of the advice in the book. I would only suggest that in my experience, it is not as easy and simple as it sounds.

All too often his examples would start with something like, "Find a house that will appraise for $100,000 that you can buy for $75,000." But it seemed to me that more often than not he was paying more than the market value in return for easy terms. That works fine so long as real estate values are increasing by double digits a year, but you cannot depend on that. On page 257, he highly recommended Wade Cook's book, *How to Build a Real Estate Money Machine*, and said it was a classic on the subject. Out of curiosity, I checked with a major book store and they told me that book is out of print, but other books by Wade Cook on the stock marked are still available.

♠ ♠ ♠ ♠

A few years ago Wade Cook made millions of dollars (or so it was reported in the news) with his real estate investment program. He said he had made millions himself with the system and he was only "giving something back" by selling his system to share his good fortune with others. Apparently, he was buying heavily mortgaged properties with nothing down, selling them with very small down payments, and taking his profits in big second mortgages. He had huge profits, on paper. He made even more money selling his system to investors looking for an easy way to get rich. (See the report on "flipping" in a later discussion.)

Wade Cook talked a good game. He had a breathless, fast-paced, excited spiel, something like the young man who appears on television selling a system for making big money with "900 telephone numbers." But think about it for a minute. Would anybody in his right mind sell you a reasonably priced property for nothing down if you were broke and did not have great credit? But if the amount of the mortgage is more than the property is worth, if the owner is about to lose it to foreclosure because he can't pay the mortgage, and if you are offering him substantially more than it is worth, that's when he is more likely to give you that kind of a deal.

But the runaway inflation (at the time) in real estate values slowed to a walk and then stopped. A couple of years later I read in the paper that Cook's real estate empire had gone bankrupt. Not long after that he resurfaced with a "sure-fire" system for getting rich in the stock market. The last thing I heard about him was that he was being sued for fraud.

I checked with our local library and found a copy of one of his books, *Wall Street Money Machine, Volume One*. One example of his Wall Street advice: find a stock that goes up and down; for example, between $25 and $35 a share. Buy it at $25 and put in a sell order for $35 a share. When it hits $35 sell and then put in a buy order to buy it again when it comes back down to $25. When you buy it again at $25 put in another sell order at $35. On the front cover it said, "Best selling author of *Stock Market Miracles, Business by the Bible*, and *Real Estate Money Machine*." Inside the back cover it said he is CEO and Chairman of the Board of Wade Cook Financial Corporation (a publicly traded company, ticker symbol WADE). I called the financial advisor at my bank and he told me that the Wade Cook stock was at six cents a share (with a U after the quote.) The 52-week high was 35 cents a share. No, I didn't buy any. (Note: I checked a few days later and the symbol was changed to WADE OB and the price was down to four cents a share.)

There was an old story of a system for buying stocks where you put the names of all the stocks on a board on a wall and have monkeys throw darts at the wall. When a dart hits the name of a stock, you buy it. Is it possible that Mr. Cook would have done better using that system instead of following his own advice?

I'm not saying that all the nothing-down advice is bad. I bought my first home for $4,995 with nothing down, as described elsewhere in this book. But that was for a home to live in, and I made my payments with the rent money I had been paying. I also bought a 12-unit apartment building with nothing down, as described in another section. But that figured to be a money machine, and I had good credit and a good job with the federal government at the time, with an ample salary to live on. Also, that deal involved a bank, a local insurance company, a second mortgage company, and a second mortgage on my home, and the seller got all cash at closing. It also required the sale of a second house I owned for the money I had to have to make extensive renovations to the 12 units in order to qualify for the permanent financing that I had to have within 90 days (see chapter 8.)

♠ ♠ ♠ ♠

If you searched long enough and hard enough you might find someone who would testify that he bought $10 worth of lottery tickets each week for five years and finally hit a winner for $20,000,000. Does that make buying lottery tickets a good investment? You could "prove" it by his testimony, but that would not make it so. Some statistician figured out the odds of hitting the jackpot in the lottery. He said buying 50 lotto tickets a week would give you the mathematical chance of hitting the jackpot once in 5,000 years, on average. I'm not prepared to wait that long.

♠ ♠ ♠ ♠

If you are looking for a serious, in-depth treatise on real estate investments, I recommend *Real Estate Investments and How to Make Them*, by Milt Tanzer, published by Prentice Hall. In 300 plus pages, he provides a wealth of information and excellent advice, all in an easy-to-understand form. He tells how to get rich surely and <u>eventually</u>, rather than preaching pie-in-the-sky immediately. If you want additional information about the book or about real estate forms you can use, you can reach him on the Internet at *www.investmentre.com.*

♠ ♠ ♠ ♠

In recent years the mortgage companies have come up with home-equity loans for up to 125 percent of the appraised value of your home. But what happens if the owner gets transferred across the country and is forced to sell? He will be up-the-creek without a paddle, as the saying goes. That might be a way out for someone who is desperate and has no other alternative. But I wouldn't sleep well if I owed that much more on my home than it was worth.

In the mid-1970s, I took a course in syndication. The instructor was a young man named Carleton Sheets. He was good, and he knew his subject. Much of the instruction was on the securities laws governing syndication and how to avoid going to jail for violating them. I don't know when he made the change, but for several years he has been appearing on television selling his book and his cassettes about how to get rich in real estate with no experience and no money. A friend loaned me one of the video tapes Sheets made to promote his courses. He does have many sound ideas, but in my experience, getting rich in real estate is not as quick and easy and profitable as the ads make it out to be. Apparently Mr. Sheets found there was more money in selling his system than in practicing it.

Nobody can predict for sure which way real-estate prices will go next. Sometimes they move against the general trend of inflation. The nothing-down buyer almost always takes on more in mortgages than the property is worth and then depends on inflation and rising real-estate values to bail him out and produce a profit. But if market values go down, he is in trouble.

That's when Pandora's box is open. In almost every case there are two mortgages or more, the original first mortgage and a second or third mortgage he gives for the down payment. Now he can't sell his property, or give it away, because he owes more money in mortgages than it is worth. He can't rent it profitably because the obtainable rent won't cover the mortgage payments. He can't let the mortgage company foreclose without risking a deficiency judgment and ruined credit for several years. He can't deed it back to the first mortgage holder in lieu of foreclosure, because he would still be liable for the other mortgages. He may have to pay taxes on phantom income. If he walks away from the mortgage debt, or if a lender forgives any part of it, IRS is likely to consider that to be income to him and therefore taxable.

He may think he can't lose anything because he put no money down. But he invests his good name and his credit rating when he assumes mortgages and signs a new one for the down payment. For every mortgage there is a promissory note, and there are ways to collect these debts even if the mortgaged property won't sell for the amount of the debts. When someone tells you, "Don't worry, real-estate prices always go up," ask him how far back he can remember. Stock-market prices have always gone up too, if you waited long enough. The Dow Jones averages fell drastically in 1966, and took 13 years to recover to the 1966 level.

About four years ago, Alan Greenspan, the chairman of the "Fed," warned about irrational exuberance in the stock market. The Dow then was around 6,000 and within the next two or three years it went to 11,000 as I recall. Now it is back down to around 8,000, and the "experts" are wondering where it will bottom out. Real-estate values go through similar cycles, although they are more gradual. Nevertheless, those who can't wait-out the down cycles may be in for trouble.

Nobody rings a bell when the stock market or real estate prices hit the top or reach the bottom. My advice is to get started, invest for the future in real estate, and be prepared to ride-out the ups and downs.

Thoughts On Home Ownership And Mortgages

CAVEAT: Remember that I am not writing this as a self-professed expert on the subject. I was born in 1920, and during the 1930s I knew too many families who had to move often as sharecroppers because they didn't own a home. Clearly, my opinions have been influenced by my upbringing during the depression. But the opinions of present-day experts may have been influenced equally by their upbringing during boom times with an ever-escalating Dow Jones index. I'm sure many of them are having doubts about their infallibility since the spring of 2000.

LESSON 36: *If you want to gamble on the stock market with money you can afford to lose, go right ahead. You might actually make it big. But be careful about putting a mortgage on your home (or failing to pay off such a mortgage) just so you can play the stock market with that money.*

LESSON 37: *Don't invest all your savings in stock of the company you work for. If it goes bankrupt, you will lose both your savings and your job.*

There are many good reasons for buying a home. Everyone has to live somewhere, and living outside or in the streets is not a good alternative. Owning a home gives you and your family a sense of permanence and security that you don't get from renting. Your taxes may go up, but nobody can raise your rent. The mortgage interest you pay can be a tax deduction under most circumstances, and so is your real estate tax. If you want to spend money to improve the place, you usually benefit from increasing the value of what you own. Whether you think of it that way or not, if you expect to own the house for a long time you are investing for the future. Generally speaking, when someone buys an expensive house with a large down payment he is a move-up buyer. That means the down payment comes from the profit on the sale of an earlier, less expensive home that the buyer has owned for a long time.

But there is another side to the coin. If something breaks you can't just call the landlord and tell him to fix it. If you own the house, it is your problem. If your roof wears out, you are the one to pay for a new one. If the lawn needs mowing or the house needs repainting, you are elected for the job. It costs money to keep a house in good condition. Water, sewer, garbage collection, and such things nibble away at your bankroll. Sooner or later you may need a new air-conditioning system or a new furnace. They don't last forever, and it's good to have a contingency fund for such emergencies.

For many years inflation has been a way of life. Because of the cost of selling a home and buying another one, they used to say you must live in a house at least two years in order to break even when you sell it. That is not always true, because sometimes prices rise very rapidly. On the other hand, many people bought homes in Maryland in the late 1980s, and had to lose thousands of dollars when they sold, even several years later. In addition to the usual sales commission, there are other fixed costs in transferring title to property in Maryland. Because of these expenses, the cost of transferring title is less expensive in Virginia than in Maryland.

♠ ♠ ♠ ♠

Occasionally, you hear of someone "flipping" a contract and making a nice profit, especially in the case of vacant building lots. For example, investor A contracts to buy a building site from lot owner B for $100,000 with 60 days allowed to settle. A month later, investor A sells the contract to builder C for $125,000, because C has just sold a house and needs another building site. Then when they go to settlement, owner B deeds the property directly to builder C, who pays the new increased price under his contract with A. Investor A collects $125,000 from the builder and pays $100,000 to the original seller. He has made $25,000 without ever taking title. But if B is taking back a mortgage from A as part of the purchase price, he may object to taking a mortgage from C instead. So if a buyer is going to try to flip a property he should play safe by including "or assigns" after his name in the purchase contract.

Flipping was prevalent during the early days of the condominium craze in Florida when builders had big backlogs of condo orders. An investor would contract to buy a condominium that was to be built and delivered in about a year. As the condominium building progressed, the price of the units often escalated. Then, when the investor was about ready to close and take possession of his new unit, he sold to a home buyer for several thousand dollars profit. The home buyer gained because he could move in right away and didn't have to wait several months for completion of a newly sold unit. When many condominium buildings were being built and prices were escalating rapidly, some investors made deposits on several condominium units at the same time, never expecting to live in any of them. On the other hand, some lost their deposits when prices flattened out and the investors could not find buyers for all the units they had contracted to buy.

The practice of flipping is less common in sales of occupied homes, especially if a new mortgage is required. There is also the problem of repeated showings of a house that is already under contract.

In my experience, flipping was considered neither illegal nor immoral. But the connotation of a word often changes with the passage of time. When I was young, we thought the word "gay" described a person who was happy and carefree. Now it means something quite different. And the perfectly respectable term "flipping" has now come to mean something fraudulent and illegal, at least in Baltimore, Maryland. The Greater Baltimore Board of Realtors has issued a flier warning buyers to beware of the practice. Although the flier did not specify all the details, I inquired from other sources and learned that the fraud involves deliberately overvalued appraisals on sub-standard houses, together with falsified documentation of applicants' ability to carry the mortgages. Lending institutions are then persuaded to lend far more than the houses are worth to unsuspecting and unsophisticated home seekers who turn the money over to the con-men sellers. The sellers then disappear, leaving the buyers with mortgage payments they can't meet and junky houses they can't maintain or sell.

♠ ♠ ♠ ♠

Real estate agents are trained to explain the tax advantages of owning a home. They can run a set of figures on a computer to show that your mortgage payment, after deducting the tax savings, will be less than the rent you are paying. Many times they include a factor in their calculations for equity buildup from inflation. Some hedge by getting you to tell them what you think the inflation factor should be. Then if it doesn't turn out that well you can't blame them. Such calculations are useful, but the promises in these projections are not carved in stone and you cannot take them to the bank.

Most of the demonstrations I have seen did not mention the standard deduction. You don't get the tax deductions for mortgage interest or property tax unless you itemize your deductions. But the standard deduction is yours for free if you choose not to itemize. I recommend buying a home as a place to live and as an investment for the future. But if you plan to buy a home primarily for the purpose of saving money on taxes, find out first what your standard deduction is and then deduct that amount from the tax benefits you expect from home ownership. Many people, especially older people with low (or no) mortgage payments, get greater benefits from the standard deduction than from the tax benefits gained by owning a home.

♠ ♠ ♠ ♠

A prominent financial advisor who has written several books advises everyone to carry the biggest mortgage they can get on their homes. He says they can always earn more interest by investing the money than what they would have to pay in mortgage interest. That has been true for certain periods of time, but not always. I believe his company also sells mutual funds and other investments. I won't say that colors his thinking, but it makes me wonder. Anyone can have 20-20 hindsight, but nobody knows which stock will take off next, or which one will go belly-up and crash and burn like many high-fliers have since the spring of 2000.

I might consider refinancing my home to raise enough for the down payment on a guilt-edged residential rental property, because the rental income would then make the payments. But the building would have to show a substantial cash flow, enough to make the extra payments on the new home mortgage and to allow for vacancies and credit losses. I would also prefer to invest in apartments that appeal to middle income tenants. Then if times get hard, some tenants of high-priced luxury apartments may want to move down to my level to save money.

♠ ♠ ♠ ♠

An investment advisor where I bank tried to persuade me to buy Micro-Strategy stock in early 2000 when it was selling for $180 a share. He said it had been as high as $333 a share and he "had a lot of it." He had followed it since it went public, he said, and he expected it to go even higher. Luckily, I didn't buy.

He liked to talk about people with "dead equity" in their homes. He said they should refinance (or get a home-equity loan) to get the dead equity out to invest in stocks, because that is the only game in town. On June 21, 2002, the Washington Post reported that Micro-Strategy closed the previous day at $1.04 a share, and the managers at Micro-Strategy were considering a reverse split in order to increase the price per share and thereby avoid being de-listed by the NASDAQ exchange. I understand that the investment advisor I mentioned is no longer working in that job.

A friend of mine told me three or four years ago that his married daughter worked for one of the Internet companies and had a lot of stock and stock options in that company. "With the price of the stock now, she is a millionaire," he had said. But the stock is now down to just about nothing, and I believe the company is in Chapter 11 bankruptcy. I have been afraid to ask if she still has a job there. In recent years the market has been in a big bubble. But you may expect all bubbles to eventually burst, and the bigger the bubble gets, the more likely it is to burst.

I'm not knocking stocks in general. I have a friend in Florida who has been active in the stock market for the entire 50 years I have known him. He really believes in stocks, and he has made huge profits over many years. He suffered heavy losses within the past couple of years, although he still has a very substantial portfolio and is far ahead of the game.

But the stock market has always made me nervous, because I have absolutely no control over what happens. I also cannot understand how they can justify paying millions of dollars in salary and bonuses to the CEO of a company that suffered heavy losses during the previous year. Then there are the stories of Enron, Micro-Strategy, PSI Net, and Hechinger's. They were all high fliers at one time. W.T. Grant also was once a powerhouse and it is now gone and largely forgotten

Even K-Mart is in trouble now. A few years ago properties triple-net leased to K-Mart were considered the safest of real estate investments. Now there is talk K-Mart may go bankrupt. But if that happens, I would rather own the real estate they occupy than stock in their company.

On June 26, 2002, WorldCom, the second largest long-distance telecommunications company in the world, announced they had improperly accounted for $3.8 billion in expenses and would take a charge against earnings that would wipe out all its reported profits since the beginning of last year. They said later that they would lay off 17,000 employees. The company may survive, but likely will go into Chapter 11 bankruptcy. The announcement said Wall Street was shaken by this announcement, and the NASDAQ hit a five-year low.

♠ ♠ ♠ ♠

Every person has the right to make his own choices, and I choose to let others play the stock market. I just feel better having my investments in something more tangible, like real estate.

"If you don't know who you are, the stock market is an expensive place to find out." Adam Smith, quoted in Parade Magazine, page 10, July 14, 2002. In the same article was an interesting quotation from Mark Twain: "October is one of the singularly most dangerous months to speculate in stocks. Others are November, December, January, February, March, April, May, June, July, August, and September." In view of the events of the past two years, there no doubt are many others who share that view.

Allan Sloan is Newsweek's Wall Street editor. On June 25, 2002, his column appeared in the business section of the Washington Post newspaper.

> "The fact that options value is not subtracted from corporate profits has led corporations to give loads of them to chief executives, who make huge profits when the stock rises and lose nothing when it falls. ... He (the president) even opposes a key reform that resident sages like Warren Buffet and Alan Greenspan consider vital to honest corporate numbers: treating stock options as an expense in earnings statements. ... At Friday's close, the S&P 500, a proxy for the broad stock market, was down 35 percent from its high in March of 2000. If you make the very generous assumption that the market will rise 10 percent a year compounded, it would take until the year 2006 for the S&P to regain the ground it has lost. Who can forget the e-mails exposed by New York Attorney General Eliot Spitzer, showing how analysts privately

disparaged stocks they praised in public? So what is most of the Street doing? Lobbying to get state regulators off their backs. Many state regulators are more aggressive than the Securities and Exchange Commission, so Wall Street wants them to butt out."

"When the market was going great guns during the nineties, corporate America proclaimed that the market's performance was proof that companies were doing the right thing and that critics of huge executive pay packages and boards cozying up to CEO's were just cranks. Now that the market's down, CEO's are hiding under their boardroom tables."

♠ ♠ ♠ ♠

A lawyer writes a syndicated column that appears in the Washington Post, and he always advises people to <u>not</u> pay off their home mortgages. He reasons that they might fall on hard times and not qualify for another mortgage to provide the money they might need for emergencies. He is a lawyer and was once a real estate broker, but I cannot understand his reasoning. What better security can a person have than a free-and-clear home? I would not suggest that anyone spend his last dime or go into credit card debt just to pay off a mortgage. But anyone who has the means and has some other money set aside for emergencies should never hesitate to pay off a mortgage just because some "expert" said not to do it.

♠ ♠ ♠ ♠

They have "No-Doc" mortgages now that require no documentation or qualifying at all. They would have to be for a lower loan-to-value amount, but what is wrong with that? If you keep, or increase, your mortgage and later fall on hard times and cannot make your payments, you will lose the house through foreclosure, or else have to sell it. For all of my adult life, as a child of the great depression, my goal has been to have a home with no mortgage. I would recommend that same goal to anyone.

It makes no sense to pay out mortgage interest that you don't have to pay, just so you can get <u>part of it</u> back in tax savings. Why not just do without a mortgage and save <u>all</u> of the interest by not paying it in the first place.

It's like the old gag.

> Husband to wife, "If I go to the sports shop during their sale, I can save 30 percent on a new fishing rod and reel. What do you think?"

> Wife to husband, "I think you should stay at home and keep your old one. That way you can save 100 percent."

I take a different position with regard to income-producing property. If you have owned an apartment house for several years, you can often refinance the mortgage and take out enough money to use for the down payment on another property that you want. The tax benefits of owning income-producing property are attractive, and your tenants provide the money for the mortgage payments. Later we will talk about leverage, which is an important concept in real estate investments.

People who are in business sometimes find it advisable to refinance a home or to get a home equity loan to expand a business or to get it over a rough spot in a business plan. Others might need money for medical reasons or to educate children. All these are worthwhile reasons. The danger comes from taking money out of the equity in a home just to spend for frivolous pleasures or for playing the stock market.

My son, David A. White, and Claudia with their three children in 1996. Left to right are Joseph Alexander (born 1984), David, Claudia, Olivia Marie (born 1986), and Melissa Nicole (born 1988). David received his electrical engineering degree at the University of South Florida after first attending Georgia Tech for two years. He works as a senior design engineer for FACTS Engineering at New Port Ritchie, Fla. Claudia is from Guatemala, where she taught elementary school. They met when David was at Georgia Tech and Claudia was visiting relatives near there. They live in Tampa, where she teaches a pre-kindergarten class at the Learning Horizons Academy. (photo courtesy of David A. White)

Unsuccessful Dealing With Foreign Investors

I was planning to remarry in June 1982. We had tentative plans to move to Florida to manage my apartment buildings, since the Hurds were leaving for a salaried job with a larger complex. But in early April I had a call from a broker in Florida who had buyers for the 30-unit apartments. With some misgivings, I signed a contract to sell it to two Englishmen representing an investment group from that country. They submitted a substantial earnest money deposit and had three months to settle. The broker was to get a sales commission of 6 percent of the sale price. In view of this, we put our plans on hold to move to Florida.

The three months went by and the buyers were having a problem with the rate of exchange between English pounds and American dollars. They requested an additional two months to settle and I granted it. At the end of the initial five-month period I went to Florida and we had a conference. The lawyer for the buyers also represented the broker. I did not want to grant any more time and said the deposit should be forfeited. The forfeited deposit would have gone half to me and half to the broker, pursuant to the terms of the contract.

The buyers wanted still more time, and their lawyer said he was sure they could settle if they had another two months. He suggested they forfeit the deposit and that I take all of it; they would put up a smaller supplemental deposit to extend the contract another two months. If they should forfeit that, it would all go to the broker. The broker was unhappy about giving me all the deposit, but he signed the agreement because he would get a full commission if the sale settled. He was the broker, so he would not have to divide it with anybody. If I did not grant the extension, he would get half of the forfeited money but that would then be the end of it.

In early November the buyers gave up and forfeited the supplemental deposit, which I gave to the broker. I was lucky it didn't close, because I did better when I sold it a few months later.

First cousins visiting. (l-r) Mariangela Lopez Garcia, who lives in Guatemala, and my granddaughters, Olivia Marie White and Melissa Nicole White, my two granddaughters. (photo by David A. White)

Strip Mining—An Expensive Investment Lesson

LESSON 38: Remember Murphy's law that that if anything can possibly go wrong, it will go wrong—and at the worst possible time.

LESSON 39: "If it sounds too good to be true, it probably is." Investigate before you buy.

LESSON 40: Don't authorize an expenditure until you have a good idea of what the cost will be.

LESSON 41: Don't depend entirely on the word of a lawyer who claims to be an expert in some field. If you don't like what he tells you, get a second opinion or do some investigating yourself.

LESSON 42: Sometimes you can lose out through no fault of your own. Conversely, sometimes you make a great deal through luck.

Tom Hurd, my apartment building manager, knew a young mining engineer in Pennsylvania. Tom had been involved in coal mining activities there and was still collecting periodic payments from a coal lease he had negotiated. This engineer contacted Tom about some coal land near Kittanning, Pennsylvania.

He said an elderly widow owned 109 acres and she did not trust coal companies. It had about 200,000 tons of strippable coal within easy reach near the surface. She wanted to sell the land for

$80,000, including the mineral and gas rights. The engineer showed us drilling records and a laboratory analysis of the coal. He said there were producing gas wells in the area but none on this acreage.

He said he could lease the gas rights within a week and we could be stripping coal within a year. The usual royalty to the landowner was $2 a ton. Four hundred thousand dollars split two ways! The thought made my brain reel.

Tom and his wife couldn't buy it by themselves and wanted me to invest with them. Her parents had money because they had collected $200,000 in coal royalties from strip-mining operations on their farm. They had agreed to advance her some money against her eventual inheritance. Tom said if I put in an equal amount, we could pay half cash on the land and not have to pay the balance for a year. By that time we could have a producing gas well and could probably be stripping coal.

I didn't have the money, so I inquired about refinancing my second mortgage on the apartments. The apartments needed new roofs anyway, and I did not have the cash to replace them. I got a verbal commitment from a bank for the refinancing, and I signed a contract to buy the coal land. We were to pay half cash and the balance in one year, plus 15 percent interest. Interest rates were high then.

I had been making extra payments on my second mortgage, and a bank promised to refinance the second for enough to pay off the old second mortgage and give me back more cash than I had put into the property originally. There would be no income tax to pay at the time of the loan because the money would have to be paid back. But after I had committed to the land deal, the bank stopped making second mortgage loans and I had to go to a private mortgage company that charged me 20 percent interest, with the mortgage to be paid in full in three years. I closed the deal on the refinancing in January 1982 and completed the land purchase soon thereafter.

We never got the gas lease. I finally consulted a professional geologist who charged me a fee for a professional evaluation of the gas potential. His report said there definitely was gas under the land, and if we drilled a gas well we would almost surely find gas. That was the good news. The bad news was that the gas from the sands in that county had been so depleted from many years of production that the gas we would find would not be enough to pay for drilling the well. He did not do any evaluation or investigation. All he did was write me three paragraphs of what he already knew and send me a bill for $500.

Dealing with him reminded me of the plumber who charged forty dollars to repair a problem in a customer's water pipes. All he did was tap on the pipes with a hammer and that fixed the problem. The customer protested the charge and asked for an itemized bill.

"For tapping on the pipes, one dollar," he wrote. "For knowing where to tap, thirty-nine dollars."

All the gas wells around there were shallow, less than 2,000 feet deep. He said there might be abundant gas at a depth of 5,000 or 6,000 feet, but it would cost several hundred thousand dollars to drill such a well. Furthermore, he knew of nobody willing to spend that kind of money with no better prospects for success.

♠ ♠ ♠ ♠

Tom went to Pennsylvania and arranged a strip-mining lease with West Freedom Mining Company. They paid us monthly advance royalties for about 18 months. They never applied for a mining permit, and finally one of their checks bounced. Soon thereafter, we learned they had filed for Chapter 11 bankruptcy. They had us tied up in bankruptcy court for three or four years. We concluded later that they never had any intention of mining the coal. They were trying to sell the company and were using our mining lease as an incentive to attract potential buyers.

After they signed the mining lease, West Freedom wrote us they were in the process of applying for a mining permit and suggested we get the timber taken off first, so they wouldn't have to bury it in the strip-mining process. Tom Hurd negotiated a deal to sell the timber, and he gave the buyers a copy of our survey. (When we bought the land, we asked the lawyer what a survey would cost and he said probably three or four hundred dollars. We told him to get it done. But when the bill came, it was $1,900. That was an expensive lesson for us.)

They cut the timber and sent us each a check. I went there before they hauled the logs to the mill, and I saw they had made a mistake and cut the timber from the property next to us. I don't know what that cost them to settle. That timber was better than ours, and they said later they would not have paid us that much if they had realized what they were doing. Their contract with us was to take all trees of eight inches in diameter or larger. They had to remove the trees by a certain date, and that date had passed. We had collected for the timber and still had it. We wanted to be reasonable, so for an additional fee, we extended the time limit another 60 days and allowed them to take everything regardless of the size.

At the end of one year, we owed the last half of the sale price plus 15 percent interest. I had the money from the refinancing of my second mortgage. Tom and Cheryl did not have theirs, because her parents wouldn't advance any more money to her. We asked the seller to extend the due date another year for Tom's last quarter of the price, but she wouldn't do it. Tom even offered her 20 percent interest, but her lawyer said absolutely not. That's when I started to worry that we had paid far too much. We talked to banks, loan companies, and finance companies, and nobody would make a loan on that vacant land. Luckily, we had sold the timber for more than enough to pay the interest for that first year.

I finally got my friends Gordon and Dora MacDonald to lend the Hurds the $20,000 they needed, based on a first mortgage and on my personal guarantee they wouldn't lose their money. They got

20 percent interest, payable monthly. After a little more than a year, the MacDonalds decided to move to California and wanted their money. There was no way the Hurds could produce the cash, so I got Jody (my oldest son) to invest with me and bail them out. He was making good money as manager of a cafeteria at the time, and he came up with his half within a couple of months. We paid the Hurds what they had to have to pay off the MacDonalds, and that left them owning 25 percent of the land. Jody and I jointly owned 25 percent, and I owned the other 50 percent. Nobody else in the world would have paid the Hurds that much for that share, but we didn't have much choice. The MacDonalds were relieved to get their money and were very grateful.

♠ ♠ ♠ ♠

I still thought somebody would eventually mine the coal, so I formed a family limited partnership to hold title to our 75 percent of the land. This would allow me to distribute royalties to the five children without having to pay taxes on it first. That was the idea behind the formation of WPW Associates. My wife had two children and I had three, so we gave gift letters to the five children for a 10 percent share each. That was not enough to incur any gift tax.

My three children (Joseph III, David, and Melissa) and my two stepchildren (Jacqueline and Stephen) would each own 10 percent of the partnership. Joseph III (Jody) would own an additional 16.67 percent because of the additional share he paid for, and my wife and I would own the remaining 33.33 percent.

Eventually, we bought that additional share back from Jody for what he paid, after it became apparent that he might never get his money back. That changed the ownership to 10 percent for each of the five children and the other 50 percent for my wife and me. We gave Jody the option of buying back the 16.66 percent share at the same price we paid him for it, just in case they ever did mine the coal.

♠ ♠ ♠ ♠

When West Freedom filed for bankruptcy, we got the name of a Pennsylvania lawyer with coal expertise from the Martindale-Hubbell publication. The creditors of the company were trying to get another coal stripper to buy our lease and pay an override to them. They were trying to salvage something, but it didn't work. Our lawyer took the position that we were helpless to do anything about it and we would just have to wait. I finally got so impatient I went to Pennsylvania to visit the bankruptcy court and talked to some people there who showed me where to do research.

In about two hours of searching and reading, I discovered that we were not subject to the bankruptcy court because our lease agreement had expired automatically. To keep the agreement valid, West Freedom had to apply for a mining permit before a certain date and they didn't do it. I made copies of the documents that proved the case and sent them to our lawyer. I told him we no longer needed him and asked him to send a bill for his services to date. He never billed us, possibly because he was afraid we would sue him for malpractice. My Florida friend Mel Fine says "If you sent a jerk to medical school, when he gets his degree he will be Dr. Jerk." The same philosophy applies to law school.

Later, Glacial Minerals submitted a strip-mining agreement to us and we signed it. It provided for a payment of advance royalties when we accepted the agreement and additional payments monthly until mining started. It also provided for an additional, much larger payment when the mining permit was issued, or in 24 months, whichever came first. The royalty payment was to be $2.50 a ton or 10 percent of the price per ton at the pit, whichever was higher. We were elated over this development. Glacial Minerals was mining over a half-million tons of coal a year at that time. Our coal had a high sulfur content and too much ash to be burned in the power plants, but Glacial had the facilities to wash the coal and remove the ash. They planned to then blend it with higher-quality coal to make a mixture they could sell.

There was a delay in these plans when someone claimed he had found Indian artifacts on our property and wanted everything stopped. That held up the process until an agency investigated and decided there was nothing to the story.

Glacial Minerals applied for a mining permit and it was issued about a year later. They posted the required bond for the reclamation of the land after the stripping was done, and everything looked rosy. They went before the Sugarcreek Township Zoning Board and got the approval they needed from them. We expected them to start work any day. We were on cloud nine! But I suppose everyone has heard of Murphy's law. Wouldn't you know this was the time for it to kick in?

♠ ♠ ♠ ♠

The coal business went into the doldrums. First one coal stripper and then another went out of business. Glacial started reducing their operations, and time dragged on. The permit was valid for five years, but it required Glacial to start operations by a certain date or else the permit would be canceled automatically. They could have applied to get that deadline extended but they didn't. Apparently they just gave up, and finally they didn't pay their monthly advance royalty payment.

I learned later they had been trying to sell our mining lease to other strip miners but without success. I called the Dept. of Environmental Resources (DER) in Pennsylvania and verified that the permit had expired and that it was too late to renew it. DER wrote me a letter confirming that, and sent a copy of it to Glacial Minerals. Glacial then wrote us and told us the lease was no longer valid. Glacial was doing a lot of business at the time, and they had spent tens of thousands of dollars in engineering studies, permits, surety bonds, and advance royalty payments to us. They were professionals in the strip-mining field, yet they lost big money on our enterprise. So I suppose our venture was not so foolish when we went into it. Pandora must have opened her box and let all the troubles out.

A few months later, I got a notice advising that Atwell Coal Company had applied for a blasting permit, giving me a chance to object if I wished. That meant Atwell was planning to mine some coal near our property. It gave the name and address of the engineer who was handling the operation for Atwell. I called him and got the address and phone number of Mr. Atwell.

Tom Hurd and I met with Mr. Atwell and one of his advisors at the property and spent a couple of hours going over it. We gave them the old drilling records and the coal analysis records. They said they were interested in mining the coal, but the quality was so low they could not pay much. We finally signed an agreement for a royalty of $1.50 a ton, because they said they couldn't possibly pay more. They paid no advance royalties either.

Three or four months went by and they had not test drilled the land. They finally said the power plant that was going to buy the coal had shut down one of its furnaces for maintenance. It would be out of action for a year, and then the other furnace would be out of action for a year. They said that even with the most advanced smoke scrubbers, they couldn't burn coal with as much sulfur as ours, so he would have to blend our coal with other coal having a much lower sulfur content. At the time, they didn't have any such coal to use for blending. In addition, Atwell had planned to use a mixing pad at nearby Kittanning to blend the coal and that facility had since closed.

I finally asked Mr. Atwell what chances we had to ever get this coal out of the ground. He guessed about 50 percent, but he didn't sound even that optimistic. I suspect he had his fingers crossed behind his back.

♣ ♣ ♣ ♣

When we bought, the engineer told us the land alone was worth what we paid for it. That was ridiculous. Even 14 years later, it was worth far less. I was a babe in the woods when I went into this deal, but I soon learned that coal in the ground has very little value, especially when it is low-quality coal. To make maters worse, soon after we bought the land the state of Pennsylvania passed laws further restricting the burning of coal with high sulfur content in power plants. That made our coal much less valuable. Furthermore, the property was not desirable for subdividing, as I learned by talking to a surveying company and the septic tank authorities.

We later learned that the mining engineer knew about this land because it had been listed for sale with a real-estate company and they could not sell it. Yet he represented it to us as a private deal that only he knew about and as the chance of a lifetime. Also, the drilling records and the laboratory analysis of the coal that he showed us were much better than the results we got when we drilled it ourselves and tested it. But by that time we had already bought the land. (DUMB!—DUMB!—DUMB!) We even agreed to give him 10 percent of the royalties for finding this "golden opportunity" for us. He then went back to the real-estate company and told them to charge a commission to the seller and wanted them to pay him a finder's fee.

Tom was furious when we finally found out about this. He said that if he ever saw him again he was going to kill him. Shortly thereafter, the engineer died in a traffic accident. (Tom was in Florida at the time, so he was not the one responsible.)

After all our problems and disappointments, the Hurds had wanted for a long time to sell the property. But I always resisted because we would have to take a loss. Finally, I subscribed to a Pittsburgh newspaper to watch the ads and get a feel for the market value. Based on the ads I saw, I concluded that the going rate for similar acreage (without mineral rights) was $300 to $400 an acre, about half what we had paid.

The Hurds needed their money, and all the WPW partners would be happy to get the cash. We listed the acreage with a broker in Kittanning and sent him a copy of the survey and the drilling records. We made it clear that we did not expect the coal ever to be mined and we made no representations as to its value.

Accordingly, we sold the land and mineral rights in December 1995 for considerably less than we paid, although considering the timber sale and the advance royalties, we didn't lose all that much.

After CPA expenses and costs of the sale, each of the partners got a welcome infusion of cash and we all got long-term capital losses to take on our income tax returns.

My grandson, Joseph Alexander White, with his prom date, Lindsey MacIntosh. He plans a tour of duty with the marine corps between high school and college. (photo courtesy of David A. White)

Selling the 30 Units—Again

LESSON 43: My father was right, if you are lucky enough, "sawdust will do for brains."

LESSON 44: Before you sign a contract, be aware of the tax consequences. If you buy an apartment building in the name of a corporation, you could lose important tax benefits.

After the sale of the Broward County 30-unit building to the Englishmen collapsed, a Mr. Liebler (not his real name) called me. He owned a 35-unit building a few blocks from mine and wanted to buy my buildings since it would be convenient for him to manage them from his office in the other property. He got my name and phone number from my manager, and there was no sales commission involved.

Because I was obligated to go through with the purchase of the coal land, I had saddled myself with a horrible second mortgage. Mr. Liebler was willing to buy the apartments for $1 million, more than twice what I had paid for them, and would pay $175,000 down, provided I paid the $125,000 second mortgage at closing. He would then assume the first mortgage and give me a second mortgage with payments over 30 years, but with a balloon payoff in 15 years.

I had taken depreciation on the building and had taken money from refinancing the second mortgage. Therefore, my new second mortgage would be 100 percent profit and taxable as capital gains as I received the principal payments. If I took that down payment, I would have a substantial capital-gains tax to pay out of the down payment. But if the buyer assumed that second mortgage and paid me a smaller down payment, I would have very little tax to pay at the time. I could wait until I received the profits later in payments on the principal. Mr. Liebler wanted nothing to do with that mortgage. I told him he could pay it off the next day, but he refused.

I hired a former IRS attorney and had him research the tax question. He confirmed in writing what I had been telling Mr. Liebler. I then gave him an ultimatum—either assume that second mortgage at closing and pay it off, or no sale. I agreed to accept a down payment of $50,000 if he would do that. He wanted the building, so he reluctantly agreed.

Interest rates were fairly high when I sold, although the old first mortgage was only 8.25 percent fixed rate. I wanted the buyer to pay me 12 percent on the second mortgage since that was the going rate for second mortgages. He didn't want to pay more than 10 percent, and we were not making much progress in the negotiations.

I offered to accept 10 percent interest if we did a wraparound mortgage, and I had to explain that to him. They were popular in Arizona when I was living there. In the 1960s interest rates had gone up to 6 percent, higher than they had been in years. Some of the mortgage companies wanted to protect this high rate and started putting in requirements that their mortgages could not be paid off for 20 years. Other companies required their mortgages to be paid off if the property was sold. Later on, rates went up and real-estate values went up, and the all-inclusive (wraparound) mortgage became popular. Some owners used it because the first mortgages could not be paid off, and others used it to try to get around a due-on-sale clause in their mortgages.

In a wraparound mortgage, the seller takes a mortgage big enough to include the first mortgage and the second mortgage combined, and takes one interest rate for the complete package. The buyer makes one payment to the seller (or to a designated third party) and the seller pays the first mortgage from the proceeds and keeps the rest. This could be a bonanza for the seller, because he might be getting 10 percent on the all-inclusive wraparound and paying only 6 percent on the first mortgage. On a first mortgage of $100,000 at 6 percent, for example, he might be making a 4 percent profit ($4,000 a year) on the difference in the interest rates. Title-insurance companies acted as escrow agents in Arizona, and they did a big business in managing these wraparound mortgages, accepting the wraparound payments and making the other mortgage payments from them. Some properties had been sold two or three times with a new wraparound each time.

Mr. Liebler didn't like that idea and suggested another possibility. He had been looking at a property in Tampa, and the seller had asked for a participation clause in return for a lower interest rate. I had learned about that in one of the CCIM courses, and I thought it was a good idea. We eventually agreed to a fixed interest rate of 10.5 percent with payments that would pay it off in 30 years, but with the entire amount due in 15 years, a balloon note. In return for this rate, he had to pay me 30 percent of all rents he collected in excess of the rent roll at the time of sale.

These payments would be considered extra interest, and this arrangement would continue so long as he owed the mortgage. If rents went up, I would participate in the profits. If they did not go up, he had an interest rate lower than he could otherwise get. That arrangement is like a percentage lease on a store. The landlord accepts a lower flat-rate rental, and in return he gets a certain percentage of any increases in gross sales receipts. The more money the store makes, the more rent the landlord gets.

♠ ♠ ♠ ♠

I was using a lawyer named Mr. Lance, (not his real name) recommended to me by a broker in Ft. Lauderdale. He prepared the contract, wrote the mortgage, and handled the closing. I think he must have charged me another fifty dollars every time he moved my file to the other side of his desk or every time he thought about the case while he was brushing his teeth, and his final bill was about three times what I expected.

Mr. Lance did not like the idea of the participation clause, and he did everything he could to talk me out of it. I don't think he had ever written one, and that made him resist it. The only argument he could think of was it might push the interest above the usury rate. I told him just to include a provision that in no case would the total interest paid exceed the lawful limit.

I finally had to tell him there was going to be a participation clause in the mortgage, and if he wouldn't do it I would get a different lawyer. I told him what to put in it, and all he did was translate it into legal language. The participation payments gradually grew from a few dollars the first year to a few thousand one year. Later the owner had some hard luck and let the property run down until he started having more vacancies. Then the income declined until the participation payments eventually disappeared.

The lawyer also didn't want to put a 15-day default clause in my mortgage. If the borrower missed a payment, that is the amount of time I would have to wait before starting foreclosure proceedings. He insisted that 30 days was customary and saw no reason why I needed a shorter default period. I told him the first mortgage had a 30-day default period, and I wanted to be able to start my action first if foreclosure became necessary. That would make it just a little harder for the first mortgage holder to freeze me out with my second mortgage. He still argued, taking the attitude that "I'm the lawyer and I know what is best for you, so shut up and do it my way." But I insisted until he made it 15 days, and that worked to my advantage a few years later. The sale finally closed on December 16, 1983. Out of the 5 percent down payment, I netted only a little over 3 percent after legal expenses, prorating of taxes and rents, and closing costs.

The buyers paid off the second mortgage immediately, but their lawyer paid the mortgage holders with his personal check, and they had to wait a few days for it to clear. They came back and demanded that he pay the interest for those days they had to wait for their money. Mr. Liebler wanted me to pay it, since I had insisted that he assume the mortgage and then pay it off. He was afraid they would sue him if he did not comply.

I studied the closing statement and found that the closing agent had made a mistake against my interest in an amount equal to about half of the interest he wanted me to pay. I wrote Mr. Liebler back and told him his lawyer had the cash in his account, and should have paid the mortgage off with funds immediately available as soon as he got the satisfaction of mortgage signed. I could not be responsible for that since I had no control over it. I pointed out the mistake in the closing statement and said I would waive my claim to that in an effort to be fair, but if that wasn't good enough they would just have to sue. I never heard any more about it.

The Lieblers wanted me to let the payments come due on the first of the month instead of the 16th. I refused, because I knew they would want to make each month's payment from the rents collected for that month. They would have to collect the rent checks and wait for the funds to be available, so every payment would be at least a week late.

I had not wanted to sell for cash, because of all the taxes on the profits. Also seller-assisted financing usually can produce a higher sale price. The buyer was putting down $175,000, including the immediate payoff of the second mortgage, so that eased my mind about security. Taking an installment sale instead would give me a huge tax break, since the taxes would become due only as the principal balance payments came in monthly.

♠ ♠ ♠ ♠

Many years ago, IRS regarded a sale as an installment sale only if the seller received 30 percent or less of the sale price in the year of sale. Thus 29 percent down became a watchword if the sale included substantial capital gains. But if the seller's mortgage was more than the remaining tax basis in the property, then the excess amount of the mortgage that was more than the tax basis was considered cash in the year of sale. I believe the rules for an installment sale have since been liberalized, but the mortgage over basis amount no doubt still counts as cash in the year of sale.

When there is a huge profit involved, an installment sale is an excellent way to spread out the tax bite over several years while earning interest on the money you would have had to pay out in capital gains taxes had you sold for all cash. At the time of sale, your accountant will compute what percentage of your take-back mortgage is profit and how much is return of your investment. Then as the money comes in each year, the interest you receive is counted as ordinary income, and the principal reduction each year is divided as capital gain or return of investment. You pay no tax on the return of your investment, and you pay capital gains taxes on the percentage that is profit. Your capital gains tax rate is based on the law in effect in the year in which you receive the payment.

A Tennessee friend of mine bought a piece of land many years ago and built a brick house on it for his home. He was a skilled brick mason and did most of the work with his own hands. Eventually he sold it for a large profit, taking one third down and holding the mortgage himself. He thought he would be able to pay taxes on his profit as he received the money over the years, but IRS disallowed the installment sale because he got too much of the money in the first year. They hit him for the full amount, and he was distraught. "If I hadda knowed I wuz gonna hafta pay on what I didn't git," he complained to me later, "I wouldn't a-sold it"

♠ ♠ ♠ ♠

Things went well at first. Mr. Liebler always carried a portable telephone with him and was usually at one or the other of his two buildings. This was convenient, since he was available on short notice to show an apartment or to answer a complaint. But then he traded his other building for a building in Pompano Beach, which was nearer to his home. This made his office 10 miles away instead of five blocks away. He lived in Boca Raton, which was even farther away. One day he fell and broke his leg, and he was out of action for a long time. His wife had to take over, but she had neither his energy nor his knack for getting along with tenants. They started having vacancy problems, and the income started to decrease.

Because of the reduced income and the high debt-service payments, there wasn't much money for maintenance. The first mortgage had a fixed interest rate of 8.25 percent but it was getting near the end of the term. The principal and interest payments were the same as when the mortgage was first placed, even though the mortgage balance was low. The Lieblers also had to make large monthly payments on the second mortgage, so his debt service payments were much higher than one might expect for the amount of money he owed. Their mortgage balances were reducing substantially, but that is a long-term benefit and does not help with the immediate cash flow.

The Leiblers had bought near the peak of the market when the tax benefits of owning investment property were at their highest. As I recall, the depreciation period then was 15 years on residential rental property, so he could take an additional tax loss each year of 1/15th of the value of the buildings. He could deduct all his expenses and interest on his mortgages and also tens of thousands of dollars a year that he did not have to pay out in cash. That resulted in a substantial paper loss on his tax return, and he could deduct that loss against any income he may have had from other sources. This was a mixed blessing, however, because the depreciation produces a phantom profit when the property finally is sold.

For example, if he held the apartments 15 years he would take 100 percent of his allowable depreciation and defer paying taxes on that amount. His tax basis would be the cost of the land, which is not subject to depreciation. If he then sold the apartments for exactly what he paid, he would owe capital gains taxes on all the depreciation he took or could have taken. The IRS considers that profit. The law says depreciation allowed or allowable, so not claiming the depreciation as a loss would not help. The depreciation taken is deducted each year from ordinary income, but the tax on the profit from the sale is taxed as capital gains, at a lower rate.

Note: If the title to an apartment house is in the name of a corporation, the deductions for depreciation that exceed rental income cannot be passed directly down to the owners to be deducted from their personal incomes. For this reason, titles are usually in the names of individuals, tenants by the entireties, tenants in common, general partnerships, or limited partnerships, all of which allow this tax break. A sub-chapter S form of ownership does allow such pass-through, but the last time I heard, a sub-chapter S corporation could not be used in connection with residential rental income.

These tax benefits drove the price of apartment buildings up to unrealistic levels. The Lieblers bought the property for an amount equal to 7.75 times the gross scheduled annual rents. They call this the Gross Rent Multiplier, and some use it to make a rough calculation of the value of an income property. It is not a reliable guide, although many use it. In the past, under more normal circumstances, a buyer of 30 units probably would insist on a price closer to five times the gross scheduled annual rents (Meaning how much rent would be collected if there were no vacancies or credit losses.)

The law regarding depreciation that is in effect when the property is put into service is what governs all during the time you own it. My depreciation period was 25 years, so when the law changed to 15 years I still had to stay with 25 years. Likewise, Mr. Liebler could stay with 15 years even though the law was changed again while he owned it.

But in less than three years after he bought, the Tax Reform Act of 1986 was signed into law and that caused the market value of the apartments to drop immediately by about 20 percent. The depreciation allowance was cut almost in half for anyone buying after that law was passed, and the capital-gains rate was increased. Also, there were new restrictions on how much of the loss could be deducted from other income, and rental investment property became much less desirable to investors. I was lucky to have sold at the top of the market.

This combination of circumstances eventually caused the Lieblers to sell the property at a considerable loss. I found out about the sale only when they asked me to confirm the principal balance on my second mortgage.

My oldest son, Joseph C. White III (Jody to family and friends). He majored in marketing at the University of South Florida and is a low-handicap golfer. He is now the golf professional at the Yazoo Country Club at Yazoo City, Mis. In addition, he is club manager and part-time head chef. He worked for several years for the Picadilly Cafeteria chain and managed several of their cafeterias before settling into his present position. (photo courtesy of Joseph C. White)

Expensive Tax Information

LESSON 45: The tax laws regarding repossession of seller-financed property are complicated and few people understand them. Most lawyers I consulted didn't understand them either.

LESSON 46: Don't assume that an "expert" is always right, just because he is a professional. Lawyers are human and can make mistakes, just as regular citizens can.

LESSON 47: Don't assume you are getting a good deal on a property simply because the seller doesn't have to pay a commission and because you are paying a lot less than the seller paid when he bought it.

LESSON 48: Don't buy an income property without a contingency for estoppel letters from each one of the tenants to verify what you have been told. At a minimum, these letters should stipulate the amount of the security deposit, the amount of rent per month, the date to which the rent is prepaid, and the expiration date of the lease.

Mr. Liebler owned the 30-unit apartments for seven years and then sold them to a woman named Lederman (not her real name). She had recently married a man who had a new real-estate sales license, and she planned for him to manage the buildings. I think she bought direct from Mr. Liebler and his wife and there was no sales agent involved. He sold the building for 12 percent less than he had paid for it, and she probably thought she got a great bargain. She paid $100,000 down, assumed the first and second mortgages, and gave him a third mortgage. I don't think she looked at more than two or three of the units, and she surely had no idea they needed so much work. That purchase was probably the most costly mistake she ever made.

Glendale Federal Bank had taken over First Federal of Broward, and Mrs. Lederman had to be approved by Glendale to assume the first mortgage. I heard that one of her relatives did everything he could to persuade Glendale to refuse to let her assume the mortgage, because he thought she was making a mistake. This was one case where she would have been better off to take that unsolicited advice.

They soon discovered that the husband was unable to manage the apartments. Mr. Liebler had used a tenant named Charles to do odd jobs and to handle tenant complaints. Charles worked full time for a management company in Boynton Beach, and he persuaded Mrs. Lederman to turn over the management to that company. The company then collected rents, arranged for needed maintenance, and paid the mortgage payments and other bills from the cash flow.

When a tenant moved out, the management company charged the owner a flat rate of $125 to ready the apartment for showing and re-renting, and they paid Charles only a few dollars an hour for three or four hours to do the work. If it had to be painted, they charged extra. About three months after Mrs. Lederman bought it, I got a letter from the management company saying they were having problems and my mortgage payment would be a couple of weeks late. I called the man on the phone and followed up with a letter. I told him I had always thought if a tenant couldn't pay one month's rent now, he couldn't pay two months' rent next month. This applied also to mortgage payments. I told him I could not let the owner's problems become my problems. If the payment was not received within the default period of 15 days, I would start foreclosure proceedings.

I asked him if he was aware there was a participation clause in the mortgage, and he knew nothing about it. Mrs. Lederman had bought that building, retained a lawyer to represent her, made a big down payment, and taken title without learning there was a very onerous provision in the mortgage and note. She learned only after the sale that there were serious problems. She never contacted me before she took title.

The building had been represented by the seller as being fully rented, but some of the tenants had moved in by paying nothing but a $50 deposit, according to reports. If the lawyer had insisted on estoppel letters from all tenants, that would have been revealed. The management company had since attempted to upgrade the quality of the tenants and the result was eight or nine vacant apartments within a month.

I don't know who her lawyer was, but in my opinion that situation was inexcusable. The participation agreement was a complete, separate page in the mortgage, and the promissory note specifically made reference to it. Moreover, a copy was recorded on the first page of the public records where the mortgage was recorded. Mrs. Lederman owned the building less than a year, and I understand she lost substantially more than $100,000, including operating losses during ownership.

Her accountant was also the accountant for a real-estate broker named Mel Fine, and they were talking one day about her problem. She was willing to give the property to anyone who would relieve her of personal liability and would also pay the real-estate sales commission. Mel Fine talked with another agent and that agent talked with a third agent who talked with a prospective buyer, a Mr. Foundas (not his real name). Mr. Foundas agreed to buy it and to pay the selling commission, but only if I removed the participation clause from the mortgage.

I went to Florida twice to try to straighten all this out. First I met for an hour with the owner and Alan Sakowitz, a fine young lawyer who was trying to help her out of her predicament. I agreed to cooperate any way I reasonably could. We reached an accord on what later became the terms of an assumption agreement for a new buyer. The next day, I met with the three agents and Mr. Foundas at his place of business. I was assured repeatedly that Mr. Foundas was a millionaire businessman and I would have no problems if he bought it. One of the agents was a property manager and would help him with his investment.

The owner would have been happy to deed it back to me, but because of the tax consequences I decided I did not want it. It was in horrible condition and there were nine vacancies at the time. I had long discussions (at $200 an hour) with a lawyer who was a foreclosure specialist, but he couldn't answer my tax questions. He referred me to a tax specialist, and he in turn referred me to another specialist in a different city; and I finally got the answers I was seeking. It cost me several hundred dollars in all.

The second mortgage I held was all profit. The interest I got was taxable as ordinary income in the year received, and all the payments to principal were taxable as capital gains. I could not use the mortgage in a tax deferred exchange for another property, because it would not be like-kind property and would not qualify for tax deferral. I wanted to know the tax consequences of foreclosing and taking the property back and of taking a deed in lieu of foreclosure.

I had called a lawyer in Washington who answers legal questions on a radio program, but he did not give me a satisfactory answer. I then called him at his office and he referred me to one of his assistants who researched it and, for two hours billing at his rate, gave me a fast answer. His $300 answer turned out to be wrong. Later, after I finally got the true facts, I wrote to him and cited chapter and verse of the law and told him he had given me the wrong answers. I never heard from him again; and no, he didn't give me my money back.

♠ ♠ ♠ ♠

I have no authority to give legal advice, but this is how $800 worth of legal fees finally distilled the law for me:

- When the mortgage is a purchase money mortgage (taken in connection with the sale of a property,) the following rules apply:

- If the mortgage is paid off, the share of the payment that is profit is fully taxable as capital gains.

- If the mortgage is traded for another property, that becomes a taxable event and the profit is taxable as capital gains.

- If the seller (mortgage holder) negotiates to buy the property back and the balance of the mortgage is used as part of the price, that also becomes a taxable event and taxes are due.

- The mortgage may be modified or extended, or the terms or interest rate may be changed without causing a taxable event. However, the note may not be canceled and reissued without creating liability for the taxes.

Section 1038 of the Revenue Code (together with the regulations) allows special treatment in certain circumstances:

- The seller may take the property back in full satisfaction of the debt without paying the tax. However, there may not be any additional compensation paid other than the satisfaction of the debt.

- If the mortgage is in default, or if it is apparent the borrower will not be able to meet his obligation, the seller may take the property back without paying taxes. He also may pay additional compensation, such as assuming a new mortgage the buyer has put on it.

■ If the seller forecloses and takes it back, or if he takes a deed in lieu of foreclosure, he does not have to pay the capital-gains tax. He may also pay additional compensation to the buyer.

However, there is a price to pay for these benefits:

o When the seller relies on this Section to avoid capital-gains taxes, he must pay taxes on all the mortgage relief he has enjoyed since he sold. In other words, if the seller owes a mortgage and the buyer assumes it and later pays it off, that is all taxable income to the seller when he takes the property back.

o It does not matter that the property may not be worth the amount of the mortgage when it is repossessed. Gain resulting from re-acquisition includes payments purchaser made on the mortgage or on any other indebtedness to which the property was subject at the time of the sale. It also includes any debts the seller was personally liable for at the time of the sale.

I was responsible for the second mortgage, and the buyer paid it off, so I would owe taxes on that amount. I was responsible for the first mortgage, and the three different owners since I sold it had paid on the principal for 12 years. I would also owe taxes on all that mortgage reduction. I wouldn't have to pay both. I would pay taxes only on the remaining principal balance of my mortgage OR on all the mortgage amounts that had been paid for me, but not on both. Neither choice appealed to me.

A Very Complicated Sale

LESSON 49: If you hold a mortgage and a note, keep the note in a safe place of your own choosing. Don't entrust it to a lawyer or an agent. The note is the evidence of the debt, not the mortgage. The mortgage merely insures that the debt will be paid. Having the note attached to the mortgage on the public records is not enough. Having a copy of the note is not good enough.

Mr. Foundas would not buy the 30-unit apartment building unless I removed the participation clause. Mrs. Lederman would not sell unless she was relieved of personal liability on my mortgage and on the mortgage she gave Mr. Liebler. Mr. Liebler would not relieve her of liability on his mortgage unless I relieved him of personal liability on my mortgage. This gave me the opportunity to get a couple of goodies myself, so I included a couple of provisions of my own:

> I stipulated that the mortgage could not be assumed by a new buyer without my written approval, but such approval would not be unreasonably withheld.

> I would have the right of first refusal on any new financing. If the owner wanted to refinance and pay me off, I would have the option of changing the terms of my mortgage to conform to the new proposal.

> The buyer would assume personal liability on the note.

The document was titled ASSUMPTION AGREEMENT WITH RELEASE. It canceled the participation agreement and relieved

Mrs. Lederman and Mr. and Mrs. Liebler of personal liability on all notes except the first mortgage. I had no control over that. It was signed before notaries public by all parties.

Consequently, Mr. Foundas took title in December 1991. He assumed the first mortgage, my second mortgage, and the third mortgage (Lederman to Liebler.) He gave a small fourth mortgage to Mrs. Lederman for closing costs that she paid for him.

The lawyer who closed the sale for Mr. Foundas never recorded the assumption agreement. That was probably because they would have had to pay several hundred dollars for the documentary stamps they would have required at the courthouse. A few years later, after Foundas sold the apartments, I got a letter from the tax authorities in Florida asking me to pay for the documentary stamps for the assumption of my mortgage when Foundas bought the property. I called them and followed up with a letter, telling them I gave Mr. Foundas an assumption agreement containing benefits to him, but his lawyer chose not to record it. I suggested they bill Mr. Foundas for the money, since he was the one who owed it. I didn't hear any more from them.

♠ ♠ ♠ ♠

Mr. Foundas claimed to be a millionaire, but he was a restaurant man and knew nothing about property management. He was in the same situation I was in when I bought the coal land in Pennsylvania, and the results were not much different.

From the beginning Mr. Foundas was slow to pay. Checks were returned for non-sufficient funds and for uncollected funds, and it was always a struggle. Within six months he was more than 15 days late with a payment, so I served notice on him that the entire remaining balance was due and payable. That was known as calling the note.

At about that time, Hurricane Andrew went through south Florida, doing massive damage in Dade County. I called someone I knew in

Fort Lauderdale to ask if there had been any damage to the apartments, and I learned there was none. I had been talking with Glendale officials in California about the possibility of re-assuming the first mortgage if I foreclosed, so I called them to tell them there had been no damage from the hurricane. To my surprise, they told me Mr. Foundas had allowed the insurance policy to lapse. Glendale had taken out a policy through some special arrangement just to protect themselves, but it afforded me no protection.

♠ ♠ ♠ ♠

I called the insurance agent and he said Foundas had been fighting with him about the amount of the premium and was trying to get it cheaper somewhere else. He had no insurance on the buildings when the hurricane went through, and there had been no insurance for about 10 days. My mortgage provided only that I could pay the premium myself in these circumstances and charge him 18 percent on any money so advanced.

I called Mr. Foundas about this. "What are you worried about?" he asked. "What is going to happen? If somebody drives in off of the street and hits the building, how much damage can that do?" Since the mortgage was already in default for late payment, and since I didn't want to either be paid off or to take the property back, I proposed a mortgage-modification agreement in lieu of foreclosure and he accepted.

This agreement required him to send all my payments by wire directly to my bank account. That let me use the money immediately without waiting for a check to clear and without worrying if it would bounce. It also required him to pay a penalty of 5 percent of the payment if any payment did not reach my account within three banking days after the due date. Further, he had to pay the insurance policy immediately. In return, I agreed to allow him to pay interest only for one year. That also worked to my advantage, because I wanted to preserve my principal. We signed and recorded this agreement and he brought my payments current. That put the mortgage back into good standing.

In 1993 the Glendale Bank foreclosed because he was three months behind with his payments to them. My mortgage was current, because he knew I would foreclose on the 16th day after the payment was due. I had to file a cross-claim lawsuit to protect my interest, as his default on the first mortgage was also grounds for foreclosure on my mortgage. He eventually settled with Glendale but they made him pay the back taxes for the previous year. Because Glendale's mortgage was so small, they did not require an escrow fund for taxes and insurance.

To file this cross claim, my lawyer wanted the original of my promissory note. I told him Mr. Lance had it. He had handled the settlement when I sold, and he had suggested that he hold it in the note safe he maintained for that purpose. I allowed him to keep it and that was a mistake. I called his office. They said Lance had retired to a remote farm somewhere in New England. His one-time partner was still there, but he couldn't find any trace of the note. We finally contacted Lance through his son, but he said if the note was not in the safe it was in my file. Investigation revealed they had destroyed all of Mr. Lance's old files a couple of years previously.

My lawyer said if the mortgage was paid off, the original note must be returned and noted in writing that the debt has been satisfied in full. A note is negotiable and the holder can sell it or borrow money against it, so it should always be kept in a safety deposit box. If a note is lost, a lawsuit is required to re-establish the note before the holder can have it paid off. If payment-in-full is offered, the note holder may not take the money and the borrower does not have to pay any more interest until the note is found and canceled or re-established. Another lawyer whose opinion I respected told me the same thing. Perhaps this rule applies only to notes held by individuals, because in my experience banks and mortgage companies do not return notes when mortgages are paid off.

Therefore, the first count in my cross claim was to re-establish the lost note. My mortgage requires Mr. Foundas to pay all legal fees and expenses in connection with collecting the mortgage, but I couldn't expect him to also pay for re-establishing the lost note. That cost me several hundred dollars out of my pocket. I thought Mr. Lance had already caused me enough grief.

I filed my cross claim in court for foreclosure against Foundas, Lederman, and Liebler, since they all were responsible on the note. I refused to dismiss the foreclosure until they had all agreed to the re-establishment of the note. After that was done and I got the appropriate court order, we also dismissed the foreclosure.

Thomas W. Tappan is the husband of my wife's younger sister, Martha, and a man I admire for his talents. Tom learned the building trade from Martha's Uncle Tom Ryon and worked with him on many large building projects in the Washington, D.C. area. In the 1970s, Tom worked as Director of Construction for the Gulf Oil Corporation in the development of the planned community of Reston, Virginia. He has extensive experience in the development of raw land into finished building lots, and he supervised the building of several home and town house communities in Maryland. As Regional Construction Manager, he also built Courtyard Hotels, full-service hotels, life-care facilities, and time-share developments for the Marriott Corporation. He is semi-retired now but often serves as a consultant to active builders and developers. (photo courtesy of Joseph C. White)

Hardball To Sell
The 30 Units

LESSON 50: Negotiating a contract is a two-way street. You cannot always have everything your way. If you demand too much, you will lose many good deals.

Mr. Foundas was always looking for a chance to sell that 30-unit property. I had told him I would consider subordinating my second mortgage to a new first mortgage of not more than $200,000. The new loan had to be from a bank or mortgage company, not an individual, and the buyer had to be strong financially. I would have to sign a document giving the new first mortgage precedence over mine (subordinating my mortgage to the new one.).

Because a new first mortgage could be for 25 years, the monthly payments would be lower than the current payments, and the buyer would have a substantial amount left after paying off the old mortgage. I offered this as an incentive to keep my mortgage in force. I was worried that a new buyer would refinance the entire amount and pay me off, because my 10.5 percent rate was higher than a bank would charge on a first mortgage at the time.

In early 1994, Mr. Foundas got an offer from a lawyer and her husband. She worked for a big developer and had strong contacts with a bank. Her father had a net worth of $14 million (so she said) and was willing to cosign with her on the mortgage. They agreed on the sale price, and she called me about the financing arrangements. The agent for Mr. Foundas had told her I wouldn't agree to what she wanted, but she did not believe him.

She asked me to reduce my interest rate from 10.5 percent to 8 percent and to subordinate to a new first mortgage of twice as much as I had agreed to. I told her the new first and my second would add up to more than the property was worth, and my position would be too weak. I would not reduce my interest rate, and I would not subordinate to a mortgage of more than I had first agreed to. I explained that if I had to foreclose on my second mortgage I could always borrow enough on the property to pay off a smaller mortgage. But I might not qualify for a mortgage like she wanted and I would run the risk of losing everything.

She then offered to reduce the amount of my mortgage from the proceeds of the new mortgage. I told her this was no incentive for me, because I wanted the income and not the cash. She said if I did not agree she would get a new mortgage from her bank and pay off both mortgages. I doubted that a bank would loan that much, but she insisted they would do it for her because she had influence there and her father would co-sign the note. She went ahead and signed a contract with Foundas to buy the property from him and applied to her bank for refinancing.

The contract was contingent on an inspection of the property by a representative of the buyer. The inspector went over each apartment and noted the smallest deficiencies. The estimated cost for all the work was many thousands of dollars. Mr. Foundas finally agreed to reduce the sale price by that amount, but that was not good enough. She wanted him to give her that amount in cash at settlement to pay for epairs. If it showed up as a price reduction, it might reduce the amount of a first mortgage she could get.

Foundas flatly refused to do this because most of the items were so minor he thought she would keep the money and not do the work. It did not matter in the end, because the bank would not loan her the money she wanted, and I would not accept her demands to reduce my interest rate and to subordinate to a larger new first mortgage. A couple of years later, it sold for 12 percent more than she could have had it for.

Payment Or Foreclosure

LESSON 51: If your property is not insured for the full value, you are self insured for the balance and the insurance will not pay you in full for your loss.

LESSON 52: If you buy a property and assume a mortgage, make sure you know what the mortgage provides. The seller may not know (or may not tell you if he does) and neither the title company that handles the closing nor the lawyer who examines the title will read the mortgage and tell you what is in it. The mortgage and note may have some very onerous provisions, especially if the note is held by an individual rather than a bank or insurance company. There could be a due-on-sale clause or a large penalty for paying it off.

LESSON 53: If you have any suspicion at all that someone may be using drug money to pay you for anything you are selling, find out for sure that the money is legitimate. If it is drug money, and if you have not exercised due diligence, the Drug Enforcement Agency could confiscate the property you are selling and you would be out of luck.

In 1994, we executed another modification agreement on Foundas' mortgage on the 30-unit buildings stipulating that payments of interest only would be paid until the entire balance came due on December 16, 1998. I suggested this modification because I wanted to maintain the principal balance at the same level. I didn't want to be eating my seed corn, so to speak. Mr. Foundas was reducing his first mortgage substantially each month, so he didn't think he needed to reduce mine also.

In August of 1994, Glendale filed another foreclosure lawsuit. Mr. Foundas was again three months behind in his first mortgage payments. When they served me as one of the defendants in the suit, they gave me 20 days to respond. I was a defendant because I held the second mortgage on the building and they had to give me a chance to protect my interests. There was a tax judgment against Mr. Foundas, so IRS was served also. When Glendale filed foreclosure, they called the note, declaring the entire remaining balance due at once. That meant they would take no more payments unless they negotiated a settlement to bring the mortgage current again. Mr. Foundas tried to get around this by going to one of their branch offices and making two of the three back payments. The branch office took the payments and gave him a receipt because they didn't know at the branch office that he was in foreclosure.

In November he called me and said his lawyer had suggested I add the September and October payments to the principal balance and thereby increase the monthly interest payment. He said there would be a hearing in court on December 16 at which time the Glendale foreclosure would be dismissed, since he had paid all the back taxes on the buildings. If I would do this, he would go ahead and make the November payment and would make the December payment when it was due on the 16th. I agreed and he sent the November payment.

♠ ♠ ♠ ♠

My daughter, Melissa, had called me and asked me to come to Melbourne, Florida on December 20 to meet her boyfriend and his parents. Further, she wanted me to come to Tampa on the 22nd and 23rd to visit with them and with her brother David and his family. I arranged with my lawyer to prepare the modification agreement and have it ready for Mr. Foundas and me to sign on December 21, 1994. Since Melbourne was only three hours from Ft. Lauderdale, I thought we could sign the agreement then and be done with it.

I drove to Jacksonville the first day of my trip, and I called my wife when I stopped for the night. She told me I had a letter from a Ms. Shafer, vice president of Rockway Title (not their real name) in Ft. Lauderdale. I asked her to open it. It said there was a contract for sale on the property, and they wanted to settle by December 31, 1994. She said they were asking me for the financial information on my mortgage for purposes of the closing statement. I called my lawyer to tell him about this development. He said the Glendale foreclosure suit was not dismissed on December 16 and I should not sign the mortgage modification agreement yet.

The next day I stopped in Melbourne for a couple of hours to visit with Melissa, her friend, and his parents. Afterwards, I drove to Ft. Lauderdale to the office of Rockway Title. Ms. Shafer had left for the day, so I arranged to meet with her the next morning. Then I drove to the diner to talk with the owner, Mr. Foundas. He said he had tried to get out of the contract, but the buyers had a lawyer write to him and threaten to sue if he did not go through with the sale. He said at least he would get his money out, and that would be a relief. He didn't tell me what the sale price was.

♠ ♠ ♠ ♠

When I met with Ms. Shafer, she assured me there was a binding contract and she was confident the sale would close. She said they could not close by December 31 because they did not have time to get the approval from Glendale for the assumption of the first mortgage. She told me the amount of the down payment, but she didn't show me the contract. I said I would answer her letter when I returned home on Christmas Eve. I asked her if the buyers knew there was a participation clause in the mortgage. She called in the title searcher, who said she did not know anything about it. I told her it was referred to in the note, which was recorded on the first page of the public record where the mortgage was recorded. Also, the participation clause was an entire page, and was an addendum to the mortgage. She said Rockway Title did not insure as to the provisions of a note or mortgage.

She considered that a matter of concern for the lawyer representing the buyers. If the buyers did not have a lawyer, then it was a matter for the seller of the property, or for the real-estate agents, to advise the buyers of the terms and conditions of the mortgage. I told her there had been an assumption agreement executed when Foundas bought, but it was never recorded. That agreement removed the participation clause and added other provisions. She said that would have to be recorded.

I went to The Family Bank of Hallandale and talked with Mr. Kier about refinancing the first mortgage in case I had to take the building back. I would need to double the amount of the first mortgage to take out enough to pay the taxes I would owe. I had planned to come back and inspect the apartments with Mr. Foundas around noon, but I canceled that because it was raining so hard and the wind was so strong. I just stopped and told Mr. Foundas it would be a waste of time because of the weather conditions. I was going to leave right away for Tampa to visit my son and his family.

When I got home, I wrote Ms. Shafer to say that if Mr. Foundas observed the terms of the unrecorded assumption agreement, he must submit to me an application package from the buyer. This would enable me to make an intelligent decision about allowing the assumption of my mortgage. The assumption agreement canceled the participation agreement, but it also gave me the right to approve any subsequent buyer so long as I held the mortgage (such approval not to be unreasonably withheld.)

If he <u>did not</u> abide by the terms of the unrecorded assumption agreement, however, that meant the participation clause still applied and he owed me several thousand dollars in participation fees. This was based on his own written estimate of rents collected, which he had submitted to the listing agent.

A few days later, I received the assumption package including a copy of the sales contract. The provisions of the contract were not clear, and Mr. Foundas told me later he was not sure that he understood it. The sale price was about 20 percent less than the property was worth, and the down payment was much too low. The closing date was December 31, 1994, but it was obvious they could not meet that date. Even a cursory examination revealed that the down payment could not possibly cover all the money that Mr. Foundas would owe at closing.

The top part of the contract stated that the buyer would assume the 1994 taxes and would assume the obligation for the security deposits and advance rents. There was a sales commission of 6 percent to pay. I had checked with the City of Wilton Manors and learned that Foundas was seriously behind with water and sewer payments. That would become a lien on the property if not paid.

There were several thousand dollars in judgments against Foundas that applied to the property, and he was four months behind on his mortgage payments. All of this had to come out of the down payment, and it was obvious there would not be enough. In addition, there was the prorating of the 1995 taxes and prorating of rents Foundas would have to pay at closing, plus other costs of settlement chargeable to the seller.

The buyers had made an adequate deposit, and the financial statement showed an equal amount in cash reserves. It showed that they had a substantial equity in an eight-unit apartment in New York State, on which they owed a small mortgage. The wife had been working in a department store and he was a taxi driver who owned his taxi.

I was concerned that they might be laundering money for a drug ring, and my lawyer told me I might end up losing everything to the Drug Enforcement Agency if I did not exercise sufficient diligence. They later submitted a settlement sheet to me showing they had refinanced the mortgage on the eight units in New York and had taken out all the money they needed. This answered the question about the source of the money.

♠ ♠ ♠ ♠

In the meantime, someone in Florida mailed me a newspaper clipping describing a recent fire that did $250,000 worth of damage to the restaurant in Ft. Lauderdale owned by Mr. Foundas. He owned the building as well as the restaurant business. I finally reached him by phone and he confirmed the report. He said he had only $140,000 insurance coverage because he owed less than that on the property. He said the insurance company would not pay him the $140,000 because they said he was underinsured and could not collect the full amount of his policy.

For example, if the actual insurable value was $280,000 and he had taken out only $140,000 in insurance coverage, the insurance company considered him self-insured for the other $140,000. Therefore, if he had a loss of $140,000, they would pay only half of it, or $70,000. He would have to pay the other $70,000, because he chose to self-insure half of the building and, therefore, had to cover half of the loss. I don't know how he finally came out with the insurance company, but that was not my concern.

I told Mr. Foundas that I had read the sale contract and the figures did not make sense. He didn't understand what I meant. I mentioned the 1994 taxes and the security deposits, which I knew he had already spent. He said the buyer was going to pay them. When I pointed out that he would have to pay at closing much more than what the down payment provided, he said he didn't fully understand it but he was supposed to come out with some money.

I thought the buyer or his agent was trying to reduce the down payment by having the buyer assume these two obligations that did not have to be paid in cash at closing. Then the effective down payment would be much less. That's why they wanted to close by December 31, so the 1994 taxes would not have to be paid in cash at closing. The buyer would have had until the following April to pay them without penalty. In situations like this, most contracts would have stipulated that the buyer would pay the 1994 taxes and that amount would be deducted from the down payment. Further, that the buyer would assume the responsibility for the security deposits and that amount would be deducted from the down payment.

The judge did not reach a decision at the hearing on December 16, 1994. Mr. Foundas had told me he had paid the 1993 taxes and this hearing was just routine to dismiss the foreclosure suit against him. Obviously other factors were involved, because the judge reserved his decision until early January. When that time came, he still could not decide, so he referred the case for an arbitration session to be held on February 2, 1995.

In the meantime, I had discovered how close Glendale came to getting a default judgment from the court on the first mortgage foreclosure, and what a predicament I would have been in if they had obtained it.

If the first mortgage was foreclosed and they had a foreclosure sale, I would be just like any other bidder. I would have to have a cashier's check for several thousand dollars for a deposit and produce the full purchase price by 2:00 p.m. the same day. But if I foreclosed my mortgage, I could bid the amount of my mortgage and would not have to have any cash.

My lawyer didn't tell me that—I had to find it out for myself. My mortgage was five times the amount of the first mortgage. The bank knew they would never be able to get the property for the amount of their mortgage, so they were interested only in being paid off. They would have no incentive to bid high enough to get my mortgage paid off also. Therefore, I made immediate plans to attend the arbitration session on February 2, 1995.

I went to Ft. Lauderdale the day before and met again with Bruce Kier at the Family Bank of Hallandale. I gave him the information on the rents and expenses on the building as presented by Mr. Foundas. He assured me I would have no trouble refinancing the first mortgage to pay off Glendale, pay my taxes, and cover all the other expenses of the transaction.

My sister, Eunice White Curtis, and I at the 50th wedding anniversary of Pete and Elrose Harper, our first cousin, in 1997. Eunice is now my only surviving sibling. Elrose's mother, my Aunt Annis, lived to be 102 and her brother, my Uncle T.C. White, lived to be 96. (photo by Joe Horton Studios)

Arbitration—Or No Sale

The following is a general review of the facts and a discussion of what transpired at the arbitration session on February 2, 1995.

The bank holding the first mortgage on the 30-units filed a foreclosure lawsuit first, and I filed a cross-claim lawsuit to protect my position. The bank refused to take any further payments from Foundas and demanded payment in full. Mr. Foundas went to one of their branch offices and made payment for two months and got a receipt. The branch office didn't know about the foreclosure, so they accepted the payment. The bank could find no record that the payment was received, and Mr. Foundas could not find a canceled check or any other record of the payment other than the receipt. He said he may have paid it in cash, since he owned a restaurant and took in lots of money; or he may have endorsed to the bank some of the rent checks his tenants had given him. The lawyer for Mr. Foundas claimed the bank nullified their foreclosure lawsuit by accepting the partial payment. (The lawyer had previously worked for the IRS.)

I had a lawyer there to represent me on my cross claim, but he never explained the danger to me. I had been frustrated in the past because a lawyer was being picky and negative, and people had told me it was because a lawyer is trained for years to anticipate anything that can possibly go wrong and to warn the client about the danger involved. After I thought about it a while, I became more tolerant. But my lawyer explained nothing to me until I had found out about the dangers myself.

He was a retired Superior Court Judge from the West Coast, and he may have thought handling a cross claim in a foreclosure case was beneath his dignity and talent. I finally concluded that he may have been brilliant in some fields of the law, but he was no genius as to foreclosure actions.

The session went on for three hours, most of it devoted to arguing back and forth between the bank's and the borrower's lawyers. After they finally produced an agreement, I refused to sign it. They wanted me to agree that I would not foreclose during the period the bank had allowed the borrower to bring the bank loan current.

Foundas agreed to pay what he owed Glendale before February 17, 1995 and would pay me all my back payments by February 16, 1995, which was the due date of my next payment. Glendale had a 30-day default period in their mortgage, and I had a 15-day default period in mine. The agreement stipulated that if Foundas did not pay Glendale within the 30-day period, the lawyer for Glendale could submit an affidavit to the court and get an immediate default judgment against him. This would mean setting an immediate date for a foreclosure sale at the courthouse and my much bigger second mortgage would be left out.

For at least a half hour, I was arguing with three lawyers (including my own) about letting me foreclose my mortgage when it went into default so I could refinance the first mortgage to pay off the bank. My lawyer even took me outside and lectured me privately that it could not be done and that I just did not understand foreclosure procedures. He said I was trying to change my second mortgage into a first mortgage and I should know I could not do that.

That was a ridiculous statement to make, especially for a lawyer, because if I got the property through foreclosure, I would still have to pay off the first mortgage. I told them all that I would never sign anything that did not allow me to foreclose my mortgage and pay off the bank by refinancing the first mortgage. If I had no rights, then why did they need my signature on the agreement?

I explained my reasons to the arbitrator, a retired judge. He commented that this appeared to be a case of the tail wagging the dog, since my mortgage was five times the amount of the first mortgage.

The lawyer for the bank finally suggested a change in the agreement that gave me what I wanted. If Mr. Foundas defaulted on the arbitration agreement, the bank would allow me 15 days to prosecute my foreclosure lawsuit before they started theirs. This would allow me the opportunity to go to a foreclosure sale first and then pay off the bank mortgage. After they made this change, we all signed the agreement.

The session took so long that the arbitrator's fee was $600. He divided that amount by three and passed out invoices to each of the three lawyers in attendance. My lawyer slid the bill over to me and asked if I wanted to write a personal check for it. I said my mortgage required the borrower to pay all costs of collecting my money, and I expected this to be billed to him. This triggered a heated exchange between my lawyer and the borrower's lawyer on one side and me on the other side. They were both ganging up on me and saying I should pay it.

In the negotiations my lawyer had agreed to reduce his accumulated fees by almost half. This covered a period of activity of about six months. In reality, he was not the lawyer I originally hired to represent me. My lawyer was very busy and had made a contract with this lawyer, a Mr. Roberts (not his real name), to handle all his court appearances and related paperwork for him. During the negotiations, Mr. Roberts had called my lawyer at his office and got him to reduce the fee.

I never did agree to pay the arbitration fee. As we left the building, Mr. Roberts began lecturing me about it. He said his services for that afternoon alone should be worth the total fee he had agreed to accept. He said I should be happy to pay the fee for the arbitration, because otherwise the bank would certainly have had their default judgment from the court and I could go "suck eggs" for my big second mortgage.

♠ ♠ ♠ ♠

When I got home, I made some calls and retained another lawyer who specialized in foreclosures. I wrote my lawyer a confidential two-page letter explaining why I could no longer work with Mr. Roberts. I said if I had not been there in person, Mr. Roberts would certainly have signed the agreement. Then when the bank foreclosed, I would have been helpless. I could not have bid because I did not have the cash, and the bank would have had no incentive to bid up the sale price to cover my mortgage. Somebody might have bought the property for a price that would have been hundreds of thousands of dollars short of paying off my second mortgage.

I told him also that during any breaks in the negotiations, Mr. Roberts and the lawyer for Foundas were swapping stories across the table about the big cases they had been involved in and the important legal precedents they had helped set. Further, both of them obviously thought I should not have been there. Apparently, mine was not the only complaint against Mr. Roberts. My lawyer terminated his working arrangement with him soon thereafter.

I sent my lawyer the fee for the arbitration session because that was a hard cost he had to pay. I offered to pay the part of his fee that he had discounted, after I either got the building back or collected my back payments, but he declined. At the insistence of the real-estate agent, Foundas paid the money to Glendale on the day it was due. Glendale then relented and said they would process an assumption package for the buyer. This took Glendale out of the foreclosure proceedings, and I told my new lawyer my default period was 15 days and I wanted him to again call the note on the 16th day.

On February 16, I drove to Nashville, Tennessee to spend a week at my sister's house so I could visit our brother in a nursing home there. He was totally helpless and my sister visited him every day. My visit was to give her some temporary relief and allow her to make a short visit to Alabama to visit her daughter and some friends there.

My wife called me on the 17th and said the real-estate agent had called to say Mr. Foundas had paid the money to Glendale that day. I called Mr. Foundas, who verified he had paid Glendale. I then prepared a draft of a mortgage modification agreement and a draft of an assumption agreement with release. I then faxed them to the real-estate agent for delivery to Mr. Foundas and the buyer for their approval. I copied the format from the earlier documents prepared by lawyers.

Mr. Fondas offered to give me several hundred extra dollars if I would wait and take my money out of the settlement. He later doubled the offer. He said if I did that, there wouldn't be enough money from the settlement to pay IRS and he could get them to remove the lien from the property. He said his lawyer would call me and explain it to me. I told him I did not like the idea but would talk with his lawyer if he called me.

I did not get home until Friday night, February 24. I called Mr. Foundas the following Monday and he was not in. So I called his lawyer, who also was not in his office. Then I prepared a fax and sent it to the lawyer telling him I refused to wait for the closing and I wanted my money.

Two days later, his lawyer called and said he had the cash in his trust account to pay me, so I should not worry about being paid. He even offered to put the money in escrow with my lawyer. I said I couldn't spend money in somebody's trust account and I wanted to be paid. He asked if Mr. Foundas had offered to pay me extra if I would wait. I told him he had offered a lot of money extra but I wouldn't take it. It sounded to me like a conspiracy to prevent IRS from collecting the tax judgment, and if I accepted money to enable it I would be as guilty as any of the others. He said he couldn't blame me, but they still didn't pay me.

The 15-day deadline for the receipt of the money in my account was March 3, 1995. I called the bank at the close of business on that day and the money was not there. I then sent a fax from my computer to my new lawyer, John A. Watson. I told him the deadline had passed and the money did not arrive. I asked him to move with all possible speed to get a judgment in default of the arbitration agreement. I also asked him how the sale would affect the default judgment, and how the default judgment would affect the sale.

I called him Monday morning. He said he had to have a notarized statement from me appointing him as my lawyer. He faxed me the document in care of MailBoxes USA. I made a machine copy of the fax (to get it on heavier paper), signed it before a notary, faxed it back to him, and mailed the original to him according to his instructions.

He called me Tuesday morning and said he also had to have an original notarized document from me to present to the court concerning what Mr. Foundas owed me. He faxed this to me Tuesday afternoon. I made a machine copy, filled in the amounts owed, signed it before a notary, and sent it by Federal Express to arrive Wednesday morning by 10 a.m.

Glendale had told Rockway Title they were approving the assumption by the buyer, and they should have the assumption package by Monday, March 13. The buyers wanted to close on Friday, March 17.

I called my lawyer Thursday afternoon and he was not there. His secretary said he had gone out of town and he would be back Friday morning. She said all the papers were ready, and Mr. Watson planned to walk them through the court Friday morning. I told her I had been trying to get him to notify Foundas that we were going for a default judgment and would no longer accept the partial payment. I called again about noon on Friday, and he still was not there. I told the secretary I was going to send a fax to Rockway Title and to the lawyer for Foundas and tell them the sale was off because Mr. Foundas had defaulted on the agreement. That got some action.

Mr. Watson called me Friday afternoon and said I could not prevent the sale and the assumption because it would make me subject to a lawsuit for interfering with the sale. He said my mortgage was assumable, and absent any legitimate concern about the buyers, I could not refuse to let them close. He said this would still be true after we got the default judgment, and the sale could occur right up to the day before the courthouse sale on the default judgment. We agreed he would go that afternoon to the court and walk it through.

I called Rockway Title and the lawyer for Foundas and told them we were going for the default judgment, but if the sale closed, we would dismiss the case. The lawyer was happy to hear that. Mr. Watson called me on March 15 and told me we had the default judgment, with a sale date of April 18. He said we had to advertise it for two weeks, and the last insertion had to be at least five days before the sale date. This gave us at least a week before we had to start the ad.

I talked to Foundas on March 15, and he said they still had to work out something with IRS to get the judgment lifted. He had to take a copy of the closing statement to IRS to show them there would not be enough of the proceeds to pay the judgment, and IRS would then remove the judgment from this property. He said it is possible they might have to put off closing until Monday, March 20

They did not close on March 17, and Mr. Foundas told me it would take about another week to get the release from IRS. A week came and went and still no release. The lawyer for Mr. Foundas told my lawyer it would take two or three weeks to get it. My mortgage was in default and a foreclosure sale was set for April 18, at 11:00 a.m. at the courthouse. No one seemed to worry because they were sure they could close before then and we had promised to dismiss the foreclosure suit if they closed in time.

They had to apply to Glendale for more time for the mortgage assumption, and Glendale extended it through 5:00 p.m. on April 14. That was the Friday before the sale date on Tuesday. Glendale had a policy that they would not allow an assumption the day before a scheduled foreclosure sale. Mr. Foundas told me he had gone to IRS three times with the appraisal they had asked for, but the person he needed to see was not there.

Foundas called me the night of the 13th in a panic. He said the man who had to sign the release went out of town and would not be back until Tuesday, the day of the foreclosure sale. He wanted me to put off the sale for just a couple of days so he could get the IRS release. I told him we couldn't do that because we would have to advertise the sale again, and the process would delay the sale at least three weeks and probably a month.

He said the IRS judgment had grown to more than double the original amount because of penalties and interest, and if they closed on Friday he would have to borrow that amount to leave in escrow in case the judgment was not lifted. He said it would cost him several thousand dollars to borrow that amount for one month from his source of quick money. (One of the agents told me that Foundas sometimes went to a city up north and came back with a suitcase full of money.)

I told him the sales commission was enough to cover the judgment, so why not ask the agent to let the commission remain in escrow until the judgment was lifted. After all, if there was no closing there would be no commission. I told him he would just have to work something out, because after six months of being put off, I wanted this settled.

When they had submitted the assumption application to me, it was the first time I saw a copy of the sales contract. When I went to see Ms. Shafer, I told her there was something fishy about it because the sale price was about 20 percent too low and Foundas couldn't possibly sell it for that price. She assured me that was the real price because Mr. Foundas had told her he had serious money problems and had no choice but to sell.

I talked with the buyer and the real-estate agent on February 3, after the arbitration session, and they insisted that really was the selling price. I knew that Mr. Foundas would have to write a very big check at the settlement table, and I had no idea how he could do it. The agent said Mr. Foundas signed the contract and he had no choice but to live up to it. I asked where they thought he could raise that kind of money. He said Mr. Foundas had sources, and he would just have to raise the money.

♠ ♠ ♠ ♠

In view of all this, I thought the sale would never close. I was not sure IRS would lift the tax judgment either. The tax lien would not apply to me if I took the property back, because my mortgage preceded it by several years. I thought when it came down to the day before the foreclosure sale Mr. Foundas might give me a deed in lieu of foreclosure. But on Friday, April 14, I learned some things that changed my mind about that.

Someone in a position to know told me the contract did not represent the true arrangements. A trust account in Fort Lauderdale held a large amount of cash to be paid to Mr. Foundas as soon as the deed was delivered to the buyer. This was purported to be in payment for the personal property that went with the apartments, including the stoves and refrigerators. Their total true value was probably less than 10 percent of that amount. I was told that some of the buyer's relatives were in it with him, and the real-estate agent might be also, and they all put up some of this extra money.

The documents submitted to me with the assumption application included a closing statement from a bank in New York. It showed the disposition of the funds from the refinancing of an apartment house belonging to the buyer. That showed the deposit to Rockway Title, which was just about the additional amount the buyer needed to close under the contract. It also showed a much larger amount paid to Mr. Foundas. I have no doubt this went into that trust account I heard about, along with other funds from the other investors backing the buyer. That made much more sense, because the property was worth a lot more than the contract price.

I concluded all this was an elaborate scheme to let Mr. Foundas avoid paying the tax lien out of the sale proceeds. I think he hoped to settle with IRS later for a much smaller, negotiated amount. The lawyer for Mr. Foundas said at the arbitration session that his client was a man who would sign a contract today and start trying to re-negotiate the terms tomorrow. (I saw a news item later that Mr. Foundas had been given a jail term on some kind of a tax charge, but I never learned any details).

In view of this, it was obvious I was not going to get a deed in lieu of foreclosure. I also heard about two investors who planned to bid at the foreclosure sale. Both of them planned to bid more than I could afford to bid. I was limited to the amount of my mortgage plus a few thousand more, and it appeared I would be outbid if it went to the foreclosure sale. I would be paid off in full, I would have to pay 37 percent of the proceeds in federal and state taxes, and I would lose the 10.5 percent interest rate I had been getting for many years. That would have been a disaster for me, so I could not afford to let the foreclosure sale take place.

On Friday, April 14, I called my lawyer, and told him to postpone the foreclosure sale, and to give Mr. Foundas time to finalize his sale. I told him what I had learned about the extra money and asked if there was any risk to me for having this knowledge. Since I was not involved in the contract, he thought I had nothing to worry about. He said if they wanted to close that day he would be available to attend the closing, but he would not tell them yet that we were going to postpone the sale. He said he would let them sweat a little more.

They finally closed at 3:00 p.m. on Monday, April 17, one day before the scheduled foreclosure sale. They used April 14, 1995 as the transaction date on all the closing papers. I got a wire to my bank account the following day for all my back payments, and Mr. Watson canceled the foreclosure sale. They combined the mortgage modification agreement and the assumption agreement with release into one document and recorded it with the other closing documents. There was a big charge for documentary stamps on the assumption agreement and Mr. Watson made sure the buyer paid that.

I insisted that the closing agent pay my legal fees directly to my lawyers instead of to me. If they sent the money to me I might have had to show it as income and pay taxes on it. I cannot deduct legal and CPA fees unless they exceed 2 percent of my income. Having it paid directly to the lawyers may have saved me the income taxes on it.

The title company called the next day to get the names of the two witnesses to my signature on the mortgage modification agreement I had signed before a notary in Maryland. They said Florida law required the names of the witnesses to be printed by their signatures, and they could not make out the names from the handwriting. I went back to the notary and got the names and phoned them to the title company.

I sent the new buyer one of my bank deposit slips for his use in sending the payment by wire each month. I agreed later to allow him to pay by check, so long as the payment got to me in time for the money to be available by the due date.

The payments would be interest only until the balloon date of December 16, 1998, so it let us preserve our principal. The first mortgage was scheduled to be paid off in May 1998, and ours would then be a first mortgage. We could decide what to do when the balloon date arrived. That would depend on our financial situation, the going rate of interest, and the law regarding capital-gains taxes at the time.

When the buyer sold the building a few years later he may have had some interesting discussions with IRS about the amount of taxable profit he had. The official records of Broward County would show that he paid probably $200,000 less than he actually did pay for the property.

The buyer told me later that he was bitter toward the real estate agent that got him into the deal. He said he had trusted him because he was from the same European ethnic background; but the agent had lied to him and tricked him in several ways. Nevertheless, he owned the property for about five years and sold it for a very nice profit.

Comments On The 30 Units Sale

LESSON 54: They say you can tell if an owner is telling you the truth about his income and expenses. Watch his mouth. If his lips are moving, he is lying. If he gives you an income and expense schedule, look for the words "Pro Forma" somewhere on it. Loosely translated, that does not mean what is, but what the owner is WISHING for.

Long before John Ruskin wrote his comment about a wise investment being worth a lifetime of toil, some oriental philosopher wrote that a journey of a thousand miles begins with a single step. My single step was the signature loan of $800 from the credit union to buy that little house in Fairfax County, Virginia when I was 37 years old.

For this recent sale of the 30 units, the seller had to submit to the buyer an income and expense statement for the previous 12 months. I got a copy of both, along with the application from the buyer to assume my mortgage. The income claimed for the previous 12 months would have required every apartment to be rented every day of the year with no credit losses. An owner once told me with a straight face that he collected 105 percent of the gross scheduled rent one year. He said the extra 5 percent came from forfeited security deposits.

The expenses shown on the report were equally unreal. When I bought it, one building was three years old and the other was four. Nevertheless, within three or four years I had to replace some air conditioner compressors and carpets. In the nine years I had them, I replaced most of the carpets, several of the compressors for the air conditioners, and the roofs on both buildings. I had to make major repairs on the pool, and I painted the entire outsides and all the interiors. I had to replace several of the water heaters, as well as some of the heating elements in the stoves. There was substantial cash flow left over, but such expenses nibble into the net profits, nevertheless. When owners tell you about their expenses, they often forget to mention many of these things, but they are real expenses nevertheless.

Apartment buildings in Florida do cost less to operate than those in the North because the owner usually does not pay for heat. Electricity provides both heating and cooling, and the tenants pay their own electric bills. Even so, a 25-year-old property such as this will have many unexpected expenses. A wise buyer will project costs for roof replacement, air conditioner replacements, stove and refrigerator replacements, carpet replacements, maintenance and repairs to the parking area, and interior and exterior painting. Some of these will not be counted as operating expenses and will have to be capitalized instead, but all will require money. Even if there is no reserve fund, these expenses should not come as a surprise when they occur.

Those reported income and expenses reminded me of the hillbilly who found himself one night at a fancy banquet. He sat between two ladies, and there was another one directly across the table from him. The tablecloth and the napkins were white linen. All the spoons and forks confused him, but when they served a cup of black coffee he knew what to do with that. He took a big mouthful and it turned out to be scalding hot. He spewed it out of his mouth all over the tablecloth and onto the white satin dress of the lady across the table from him. Then he wiped his mouth and his chin with his hand and said, "A lot of dern fools woulda' swallered that!"

♠ ♠ ♠ ♠

Anyone buying apartments should allow at least 5 percent for vacancies and credit losses. When an apartment building never has a vacancy, the rents are too low. This means tenants rarely move out, and when they do someone is always ready to move in immediately without waiting for the place to be cleaned and redecorated. If the rents are about what the market will bear, there will be some vacancies from time to time. This is a healthy situation and no cause for concern. There will be more income at the end of the year than there will be if the rents are so low there never is a vacancy. But sometimes the owner cannot raise the rents because of rent control.

Most sophisticated investors demand at least the two previous years' income tax returns from the seller, or at least that portion relating to the income and expenses for the apartments. Owners are not likely to overstate their income or to understate their expenses to the IRS. But some sellers prepare false income tax returns and give them to potential buyers. A careful investor will prepare estimates of what the income and expenses should be for a similar building. If the figures on the tax returns don't make sense, he won't trust them. If he deems it important enough, he can get official copies from IRS of the pertinent parts of the actual returns, if the taxpayer will sign a permission form. If the seller refuses to allow it, that should be a red flag to the buyer.

For a smaller project, a seller rarely shows any expense for management. That's because he or she does all the work and does not have to pay anybody. But when a buyer is figuring the net return on the investment, he should consider management. A seller may spend 500 hours of his time during the year on various management and custodial duties around the project, and ignore that when calculating his net profit. If he is fully retired, if he enjoys the work, and if he places no value on his time, he can kid himself that management costs nothing. But he is earning that extra money by his efforts, whether he admits it or not.

Joe Poffenberg told me he once bought an apartment building and converted it into condominiums. He spent the better part of a year on the project, and thought he had done well in the process. Then he realized he had been too busy to do his regular work, and his brokerage commissions had almost disappeared during that year. After deducting his lost commissions from his profits, his conversion project was not so successful.

♠ ♠ ♠ ♠

To summarize my good fortune, a small beginning investment of $800 borrowed from a credit union grew to an installment-sale mortgage having a principal balance in middle six figures. Over the period of years since the sale, there were interest payments of more than one-and-a-half times the original mortgage. Before the mortgage was finally paid off in 2000, the federal tax on capital gains was lowered to 20 percent, but the Maryland tax stayed the same. Recently I saw an ad by an investment company: "The only thing worse than dying" it said, "is outliving your money." That's why I wanted to stretch out these payments as long as I could and conserve the principal to the fullest extent possible.

But at the owner's insistence, we signed a mortgage modification agreement as of December 16, 1997 to change the payments to a 10-year, fully amortizing mortgage at 8.75 percent. That was the best I could do, but it was far better than having him refinance somewhere else and pay me off. We had already collected 10.5 percent interest on that money every year for 14 years, so I thought I should not be too greedy.

I consulted a lawyer who specializes in estate planning and we created a revocable living trust to have the shares of this mortgage, upon my death, go one-half to my three natural children and one-half to my wife. We assigned the mortgage and the note to the trust and recorded the assignment on the public records of Broward County. Thus when I die, they will not have to wait a year for probate before they can use the proceeds from the mortgage.

In the year 2000, the owner sold the property and the new buyer refinanced. They sent me a mortgage satisfaction to be recorded when they sent me the money, but they made the document to be signed by me personally. I sent it back and reminded them of what I had previously told them, that the title to the mortgage and note was now in the name of the Joseph C. White Revocable Trust, and I was the <u>trustee</u>, not the owner. They made the necessary change and sent me the new document. I signed it and sent it to the title company to be held in escrow until the money was paid. My mortgage was paid off, and I got a wire transfer for a huge deposit to my bank account

(top) Barbara Tappan Black is my wife's niece. She met her husband, Jeff, when they were students at the Culinary Institute of America. They are highly skilled chefs, and they are astute in matters of business. They own two restaurants, Addies in Rockville, Md. (named for Jeff's late grandmother), and Black's Bar and Kitchen in Bethesda, Md. Both restaurants serve gourmet food and receive consistently high ratings. (bottom) The Blacks have two young sons, Simon Alexander (left) and Oliver Pierce. (photos courtesy of Barbara Tappan Black)

Remembering To Estate Plan

*LESSON 55: Estate planning is critical where there are children
and stepchildren. Don't leave it to chance or to the intestate laws
of your state. Someone's children may be left out. A revocable
living trust is an ideal way to avoid the expense and time delay of
probate. If your regular lawyer advises against it, he may be
unfamiliar with the process. OR, he may not want to give up the
fees and costs he hopes to make by probating your will. Go to a
lawyer who specializes in estate planning. You don't want to pay
some lawyer hundreds of dollars an hour to read up on how to do
what you want done. Making the trust document is not enough.
You also must transfer assets into the name of the trust in order
for them to be distributed according to your wishes.*

*LESSON 56: Don't blindly take the advice of an investment
advisor, especially if following that advice will only make money
for him.*

Estate planning is simpler if the estate is not very large and if the
only children belong to both parents. One spouse can leave
everything to the other and depend on the surviving spouse to
leave it to the children eventually. Of course it doesn't always
work out that way. There may be subsequent marriages, or other
factors may come into play. But things are much more complicated
when each spouse has children from previous marriage(s).

The title to homes in Maryland and many other states are usually
held in one of four ways:

Estate by the entireties is the most common. It is
automatically assumed in the case of married couples

unless a different ownership is specified, and it is available only to married couples. It gives each spouse equal ownership, with the title going automatically to the surviving spouse if one dies. No probate is required, just the recording on the public records of the death certificate. If a judgment is obtained against one of the spouses, it is not effective against the title to the property, because the interest of one spouse cannot be separated from the other.

Joint Title With the Right of Survivorship (JTRS) is usually used by two people who are either closely related or close friends, but not husband and wife: such as brother and sister, parent and child, or gay lovers, for example. Probate is not required, and title passes to the survivor upon the recording of the death certificate of the decedent.

Tenancy in Common is a useful device when each owner wants to keep his or her estate separate for inheritance purposes. The ownership can be 50/50, 40/60, 90/10, or any other combination. The owners could be anybody, even people who don't know each other at the time of purchase. Each owner is free to sell that share to anyone else at any time without the permission of the other, But as a practical matter, a part ownership is usually harder to sell. When one owner dies, that share goes to his or her heirs according to a will, a trust, or the state Laws of Intestate (without a will) Succession, as the case may be.

Sometimes a married couple will have the title to the family home in the name of one spouse only, usually for purposes of estate planning. Then the owner spouse may leave the property, upon death, according to his or her wishes, subject only to any rights state laws may give to the surviving spouse. If the owner spouse should sell, however, a buyer will usually require the non-owner spouse to also sign the deed, in order to convey any residual rights he or she might have under state law.

Under Maryland state law, if one spouse dies without a will or other legally binding provisions, the estate goes to the surviving spouse. Then when the surviving spouse dies, the entire estate goes to the natural children of that spouse. I understand that is also true in many other states. The children of the first spouse to die are stepchildren, and they get nothing. In the order of inheritance, stepchildren rank behind brothers and sisters, aunts and uncles, parents, and even behind grandparents. The services of a lawyer who specializes in estate planning is a wise investment. It is an absolute must if there is a your-kids, my-kids, and our-kids situation. Don't let your Uncle Bud or your Cousin Willie do that kind of estate planning for you just because they are divorce lawyers, criminal lawyers, or corporation lawyers, even if they will work for nothing.

It's easy to say that you trust the surviving spouse to do the right thing concerning the stepchildren, but nobody knows what may come to pass in the years before it becomes an issue. If there is a significant estate to be divided, enormous pressures may be brought to bear, one way or the other. The surviving spouse may remarry and then die, leaving everything to the new spouse. Or, he or she may fall into a disagreement with the stepchildren and decide to have nothing more to do with them. Also, as more and more years pass since the death of a spouse, and as the stepchildren grow up and move away, the resolve to do what is right by the stepchildren is likely to fade.

If there is a large estate, the matter of inheritance taxes may come into play. There are ways to minimize their impact, but we don't have to be concerned with that.

♠ ♠ ♠ ♠

Now back to my situation.

I owned the apartment building in my own name after my divorce in 1978. The separation agreement gave my ex-wife a substantial percentage of my government retirement annuity for as long as we both live, with the cost-of-living increases included. She gets a government check each month, just as I do. She also got the home in Hollywood, Florida and whatever was in our joint savings account. In return she gave me a quitclaim deed for her interest in the apartment building. We still owed a lot of money on it, so it seemed like a fair arrangement.

Three years later, after I came to Washington to work, I was invited to a meeting of Executive Women International because they had scheduled a speaker I wanted to hear. There I met Linda Pumpaly, one of the executive women. About a year thereafter, we married. I still kept the building in my name, because I wanted to make sure my three children got a fair share when I died. On the other hand, Linda wanted to make sure her two children would not be left out if she died first. I attended some estate-planning seminars and consulted two different attorneys who specialized in estate planning. Finally, several years later, we came up with the following plan:

I signed a deed giving my share of the home to Linda, as sole owner, subject to the existing mortgage. She made her will leaving me a life estate in the house. I could stay in the house as long as I lived (or as long as I wanted to) in the event she died first. Upon my death, the house would then go to her two children, in equal shares. She had sold her town house after we married, and she put all the proceeds into the house and furnishings we bought together.

When I went to our family lawyer to discuss a revocable living trust, he did not want to do it. He said we would be much better off using regular wills. Most of his law practice was in family law, primarily wills and probate procedures, so his opinion was to be expected. But I had attended a series of lectures at night on estate planning, and I already knew the pros and cons. Also, I had heard too much bad advice over the years, so I went to Gary Altman, a lawyer in Rockville, Maryland who specializes in estate planning. He also recommended, and prepared for me, a living will, a durable power of attorney, and a regular will.

When I made the revocable living trust, I assigned the mortgage and note on the apartment house to the trust. The trust stipulated that, upon my death, the income from the mortgage would be divided equally—one half to my wife and the other half in three equal parts to my three natural children. It would then be up to her to disburse her share to her children upon her death, if that was what she wanted. I put no other assets into the trust, because it is strictly to control the money from the mortgage and nothing else. I also did not want a "pour over" will to put any unexpected windfalls into the trust. My three children will get half of the mortgage money and my wife will get the other half plus everything else that we own.

Monthly payments were coming in from the apartment-house mortgage, so we set up a ledger to keep a record. Every time we received a payment to the trust on the apartment house mortgage, we calculated how much that payment reduced the principal balance of the mortgage. Then we applied an equal amount as an additional principal payment on our home mortgage. We kept the interest to use for family expenses. Those additional mortgage payments were charged to her half of the trust, because the house was then in her name alone.

When the apartment house mortgage was finally paid off, it was all taxable profit so we set aside enough money in safe investments to pay the capital gains taxes (state and federal) when they came due. These temporary investments were in both of our names, because if one died the other would still have to pay the taxes. We used what was left of my wife's half to finish paying off the mortgage on the house, and gave her the rest of it in cash. She bought a long-term CD with most of it, and with the remainder she opened a checking account in the same bank in her name alone, so the monthly interest payments would be deposited automatically into that account. Both the CD and the checking account were made payable on her death to her two children.

I gave my three children $10,000 each as a tax-free gift, which was deducted from their half of the trust. I revised the trust to remove my wife's name, since she already had all of her half. Also, when I am gone she will get the standard survivor's annuity from my government pension, with cost of living adjustments, for as long as she lives.

I opened a special account a local bank in the name of the trust, with my name as trustee and my older son as alternate trustee. All of the remainder of the half for my children went into that account. Now if I die, all that money goes to them in equal shares without having to wait for probate. The bank has a copy of the trust agreement, as does my lawyer and the alternate trustee.

All of the trust money in that account now consists of a very small amount of cash and a bond that pays interest semi-annually into the trust account. The bond can be called and paid off in three years if they choose. Otherwise it is payable at face value in August of 2015. In the meantime, the cash value of the bond will fluctuate according to the prevailing interest rate, and my heirs might be faced with a decision as to whether to sell the bond at a discount or to wait and collect the interest every six months until 2015 and then redeem it at full price. On the other hand, I hope to still be around until then.

The investment advisor at the bank swore to me that the interest on the bond was exempt from state income taxes, and even made a special telephone call to his headquarters to confirm it. But he was wrong, and now it will cost us an extra several hundred dollars a year in Maryland State Taxes. I should have consulted a tax expert first, but I probably would have bought the bond anyway if I had known that in advance. "It's OK to trust the dealer, but cut the cards anyway," someone once said.

I made the trust revocable, because there is always the possibility that one of us will have to spend several years in a nursing home, and that can cost $40,000 or $50,000 a year (maybe even more) in this area. Something like that could wipe out all our savings before long. That's why I gave my three children the $10,000 each in advance. They all made good use of it, and I wanted to be sure they would get something, regardless of what may happen in the future.

I have explained to my children that we expect to spend the interest from the trust to supplement our income, which has been drastically reduced since the mortgage was paid off and we had to pay 28 percent of it in federal and state taxes. But with no mortgage payment on our home, we make out fine.

♠ ♠ ♠ ♠

We have a lovely home in a good neighborhood and we have good used cars that we are satisfied with. We use credit cards for convenience only, and we never carry over a balance to the next month. We plan to use the interest from the trust to help with our state and federal income taxes, the real estate taxes on our home, and the insurance on the house and our cars.

What we have is peanuts compared to many others. But when I was picking cotton and cleaning out stables on a Tennessee farm 65 years ago I didn't think I could ever be this independent financially. I am reminded of the thought expressed in the poem *The Village Blacksmith*: "He looks the whole world in the face, for he owes not any man."

"There is no dignity quite so impressive. and no independence quite so important, as living within your means." (Calvin Coolidge, quoted in the Parade Magazine, page 10, July 14, 2002.)

Investing in real estate made it all possible

My stepdaughter, Jacqueline, with her husband, Frederick Davis. Fred is executive vice president of MedStaff Carolinas and is president of Vita Medical Staffing. He is a graduate of the United States Naval Academy at Annapolis, Md. After that, he went to Aviation Indoctrination, Naval Air Station, Pensacola, Florida, Training Squadron 10 and Training Squadron 86, NAS, Pensacola. During the Gulf War, he flew the S3, a carrier-based, anti-submarine and anti-surface airplane. He resigned his naval commission as a Lt. Commander to join MedStaff Carolinas. Jackie is a graduate of Trinity College in Washington, D.C., and is currently attending the University of South Carolina Law School. She is the former executive director of the Womens Bar Association of the District of Columbia. They are expecting their first child in January 2003. (photo courtesy of Jacqueline Davis)

Epilogue, And Final Lesson

LESSON 57: Don't buy a building lot in a retirement community unless you are almost ready to start building and unless you can be sure the community will actually be built. There are hundreds of vacant lots, perhaps thousands, in proposed retirement communities all over the country that can't be sold at any price.

LESSON 58: Don't buy vacant land for investment unless it produces income, or unless you will soon have use for it, or unless you have reason to believe it is in the path of development. Otherwise, the taxes, the carrying charges, and the loss of income on the money invested will usually cost you more than the eventual profit.

LESSON 59: Beware of time shares. As investments, they have a miserable history.

I got the phone number from information and talked with John Elam at his home in Richmond, Virginia. He is still licensed as a real estate agent, but he is mostly inactive since he is nearing 70. He remembered the six units he helped me buy in 1966 at 706 North Belmont Street and he remembered the 12 units I bought later at 3004 Monument Avenue, which I converted to 18 units. He remembered that I paid $55,000 for that one and said it is now worth $300,000.

"Why didn't you keep it," someone might ask.

There are good reasons. It has been nearly three decades since I sold Monument Avenue. Long-distance management is a problem even when you lease by the year and have good tenants. The problems are magnified many times over when you rent furnished apartments by the week, as I found out when I moved to Washington in 1970. And when I sold it, I was living in Florida and never expected to live this far north again.

Another reason I sold was for more leverage—increasing my cash flow and pyramiding my equity (see Chapter 7). I took the money from the sale and made the down payment on 30 units in Florida. During the nine years I owned those apartments, they increased in value more than a half-million dollars. Later, there was a down market for commercial properties for a few years after the tax laws were changed in 1986, but that property is probably now worth 40 percent more than I sold it for. I have been fully retired since 1986. And as I have grown older, I have been content to enjoy the profits from previous investments and the interest on my mortgage without having to be concerned with daily management matters.

♠ ♠ ♠ ♠

John Elam told me he once showed a customer an apartment building in Richmond, Virginia that could be bought for $30,000. The customer later called him and told him to write the contract and bring it by his house the next day. When he got there with the contract, the man was sick in bed and was having second thoughts. He didn't want to sign and wanted to think it over some more.

"It was worth the money yesterday when you decided to buy it." John told him, "and it is still worth the money now. Go ahead and sign the contract, and you will feel better tomorrow." The customer bought the building, enjoyed the cash flow from it for 25 years, and sold it for nine times what he paid for it.

♠ ♠ ♠ ♠

On the other hand, Grandpa's farm in Tennessee with 30 acres and a house and barn sold for $800 in 1941 and has not changed much. A subsequent owner replaced the wooden house with a small brick bungalow, but the old barn is still standing. No one is farming the land because the topsoil is too thin for productive farming. For several years it was planted in orchard grass and cattle were grazing on it, but now nothing seems to be going on.

The town of Lawrenceburg is six miles away. It had 3,000 population in 1934 when I started high school there, and it has perhaps 12,000 now, nearly 60 years later. The population of Lawrence County is now approximately 40,000. Everything there looks newer and more modern, but the growth has been slower than in many other parts of the country. The Murray bicycle plant is still there, but they make lawn mowers, snow blowers, and a few other things instead of bicycles. Many of the local people worked there from the beginning to the end of their working lives.

♠ ♠ ♠ ♠

The conventional wisdom is that vacant land is not a good long-term investment unless you have some particular use in mind. The tax man comes around every year and there is no income unless you can rent it for some use. The value can go up very slowly, as was the case with the 30 acres in Tennessee. Every now and then I read about somebody who bought a vacant lot in a proposed retirement community with the intention of building a home on it in a few years. All too often the project did not take off, and they were stuck with a building lot that they couldn't even give away.

But in some cases vacant land has produced spectacular profits. During the great depression the Graham family bought up many acres of land in South Florida for their dairy cows to graze on. Much of it they bought for almost nothing. Then people kept coming to Florida to live, and eventually that land became valuable for building sites. The old Graham Dairy Farm is now covered with expensive homes and shopping centers, and one of the heirs to that fortune is serving in the U.S. Senate. But they didn't buy that vacant land just to speculate. They had a use for it, and it produced income for them while they held it.

The wife of someone at the association where I worked for a few years was persuaded to buy 10 acres in Scottsdale Arizona in the 1960s. Her husband wasn't interested, so she used some money she had from a previous marriage. The parcel was 40 acres and she bought it for $1,000 an acre. Three others went into the deal with her, taking 10 acres each. It was in the path of development, and the area was booming. Some 20 years later someone wanted to build a hotel or some other big project there and bought out the other three. My friend held out until the last, and finally sold her $10,000 investment for one million dollars. But this does not routinely happen. Once in a while someone in Las Vegas puts a silver dollar into a slot machine and hits a $500 jackpot. And someone may buy a dollar lottery ticket and win a fortune. But that does not make slot machines and the lottery good investments.

♠ ♠ ♠ ♠

The time-share promoters will tell you that for the one-time investment of a certain amount of cash you can have a week or two weeks each year at some fancy resort. But sooner or later you would like to go somewhere else instead and you try to sell your shares. Unfortunately, there is almost no market for them. They were very popular a few years ago when they first came on the scene. But most people soon learned that there were other expenses to be covered, and the deal was not as sweet as it appeared.

Robert Bruss is an attorney who writes a syndicated column on real estate that appears in the Washington Post newspaper. He wrote recently, in answer to a letter, that it is virtually impossible to sell time shares for anything near the original purchase price. If you want to buy one, purchase it on the resale market at one of the many web sites for as little as 10 percent of the original price.

♠ ♠ ♠ ♠

I went back to Richmond in July of 2002 to take pictures of the properties I once owned there more than 30 years ago. John Elam, the real-estate agent who sold me 906 North Belmont, met me at the building and let me take his picture there.

The building looks rock solid, and it will probably look equally good a hundred years from now. I might have kept it many years longer, but I bought the 12-unit building a block away. Absentee ownership multiplies management problems and institutional management is not cost effective for small properties. Also, I had a growing family and the profit I made on the sale gave my family a welcome improvement to our standard of living.

The building at 3004 Monument Avenue also looked as good as it did when I moved away from Richmond. It too is solid brick. I sold it to get the down payment for the 30 units in Florida. Moving up to a bigger complex gave me the leverage to get more annual operating profit, a better tax shelter, and a larger capital gain when I sold.

If I had been younger and more aggressive, I might have traded the equity in the 30 units (tax deferred) for a down payment on a 60 or 80-unit complex. That would have built wealth faster. But I was well into my sixties when I sold and was recently remarried, so a long-term installment sale with a good interest rate on a substantial mortgage was more appealing in my situation

I was ready to enjoy my good fortune and let someone else worry about. management. With an installment sale, I deferred the payment of taxes on most of my profits for 17 years after the sale, while collecting 10.5 percent interest for 14 years and 8.75 percent for three years.

♠ ♠ ♠ ♠

FINAL LESSON: Happiness comes from knowing when you are well off.